WHAT OTHER

The awakening in our day of what Christ's kingdom is all about is the larger backdrop against which I am happy to watch Jon Zens move into this situation with his theological scalpel and dissect the salient issues for us—as God is piecing them together again the way they should have been from the beginning. If women find yet again their place in the Kingdom, they will not need to be emancipated, because they are liberated. They will not want to pursue equality, but function in partnership. And no real man will be threatened by this.

—Wolfgang Simson, author of *Houses That Change The World* and *The Starfish Manifesto*

Jon Zens is a champion of women in the Kingdom—and he uses the Scriptures to prove his point. Drawing from his extensive Biblical and historical research, Jon, with clarity, insight and integrity, exposes the way controversial verses have been misunderstood and reveals a more accurate understanding. This book is a great resource for the church.

—Felicity Dale, author of *An Army of Ordinary People*, Austin, TX

Over the last two years no one has impacted me more than Jon Zens. This can be attributed to his practical yet biblically faithful style and his patience, kindness, gentleness and friendship. I know this work will not silence the critics, but my hope is that it will stir deeper reflection among the inquisitive. I have struggled with the gender issue for two reasons. Firstly, because I want to be biblically faithful, and secondly because I don't want to silence half of the priesthood. I have come to the conclusion that I would be unfaithful to both if I agreed with those who silence women. I recommend this book to every one with a hearing ear. This book has deeply moved my heart in the midst of my struggles.

—**Lionel Woods**, Financial Analyst (www. lionelwoods.net), Grand Prairie, TX

For those of us who are not biblical scholars, properly interpreting the Bible about a woman's role in the church can be tricky. Jon Zens has used his scholarly skills to bring some clarity to the topic. I hope Christians in the house church movement will read this book and see women launched into their God-given ministries!

—**Rad Zdero**, Ph.D., author of *The Global House Church Movement* editor of *Nexus: The World House Church Movement Reader*, Canada

As the beneficiary of one wife, four mature daughters, six mature granddaughters and three immature great-granddaughters, life in context has overcome gender and authority dogmas. The toilet seat in our house is down! Even as Jesus is the prototype for intercession as recommended in verses 1-8 of 1 Timothy 2, we [the ekklesia] are privileged to model what follows: *modesty, propriety, moderation and submission to Him*. Jim Watt adds a vital insight: "Fulfillment of *heavenly antitype* does away with *earthly type.*"

—**Don Atkin**, moderator, A Global Communion of Apostles, Matthews, NC

In this enlightening expose, Jon Zens takes the reader beneath the pervasive cultural misunderstandings regarding the role of women in the church and zeroes in on the historical roots of the often deplorable mistreatment of one half of the Body of Christ. This passionate, well-researched work is not only a fair treatment of the subject, but one that is biblically sound, drawing from the entirety of the Word of God. Intelligent, captivating, covering new ground—a must read!

—**Stephanie Bennett**, Ph.D.
Palm Beach Atlantic University
W. Palm Beach, FL

This book on women is really outstanding, the best I have seen.... Once again, you have been instrumental in giving me some treasures from the Lord!

—**Jay Ferris**, Bostic, NC
Author with Lisa Weger of *Not Left Behind:*
Going Back for the Offended

I really liked this study. I thought it was needful for those who cling to the notion of male superiority and dominant authority structures. When all is said and done, the spirit-filled submission mentioned in Ephesians 5 is the antidote for top-down authority and dominance. I'm still learning what it means to submit to one another in the power of the Spirit.

—**Bruce E. Newkirk**,
Ret. Federal Prison Chaplain

In *What's with Paul and Women*? Jon Zens steps up to the plate as an advocate for women. He does not skirt issues that have long held women in reins. He addresses specific Scriptures in a frontal challenge, which calls forth an accurate and responsible interpretation consistent with the Spirit and Lord of the church, rather than the continuation of cultural and oral traditions. This book will free both women and men. The two are one in Christ Jesus and are meant to co-labor in the Spirit in whom there is neither male nor female. In Joshua 17:3-4, Zelophehad's daughters requested an inheritance among their brothers, which the Lord had commanded Moses. Job's daughters are also given an inheritance among their brothers in Job 42:13-15. This same heart's cry can be heard from women today who have inherited all things in Christ along with their brothers, and who long to express this inheritance on earth as it is in heaven.

—**Christie Moore**, author of
Prophetic Words for Your Life,
international speaker/prophetic teacher,
Hazelton, Idaho

Even though I long ago settled the issue of biblical equality for women in both my personal life and my role as a pastor, I must admit that my convictions still allowed room for other believers to hold the traditional hierarchical interpretations. But Jon's thoroughly researched, historically outlined, and biblically consistent treatise for biblical equality has energized me now to take a clear and resolute stand against the traditional position that sins against Christian sisters and women in general. Jon boldly proclaims in his conclusion, "It is time for honest Bible students to revisit 1 Timothy 2:11-15 and to separate reality from fiction."

—**Dr. Ken Fong**, Senior Pastor,
Evergreen Baptist Church of Los Angeles,
Rosemead, CA

This is an important book. It provides new insight into a topic which has sadly divided the Church for much too long. I have been greatly enlightened by the work Jon has done in this book and I strongly recommend it to everyone who takes God's Word seriously.

—**Keith Giles**, Orange, CA Subversive1.
blogspot.com; author of *The Gospel:
For Here Or To Go?*

Jon Zens is one of the church's best kept secrets today. This little book presents a colossal challenge to years of subjugating women in the name of Christ. It is a theological bulwark against those who would use the New Testament to teach a second-class citizenship for females in the kingdom of God.

—**David D. Flowers**, free-lance writer & blogger, The Woodlands, TX

Jon does an exemplary job in explaining Paul's writing about women in 1 Timothy 2. It is a thorough and complete examination of Scripture in the context of Ephesian culture and history. Jon disbands and systemically dismantles many restrictions that stifle the God-given ministry gifts of women to the Body of Christ. If you've made up your mind or are still wondering whether women belong in ministry, this is a must read.

—**Antonia Clark**, co-laborer at New Bethel Community Church, Buffalo, NY

Your study on 1 Timothy 2 is the most thorough exposition I have ever seen. My thinking has been along similar lines.

—**Alan Crandall**, past Edwin Lindsay Chaplain to Students University of Dubuque, Iowa

This is a well researched and documented book, not based on opinion but on Biblical truth. Jon brings freedom to both women and men. His book sets women free to use their God given gifts in the church. It also relieves men of the pressure to have all the gifts and all the answers. I believe that this book will become a classic on the subject.

—**Jan Walter**, TEAM Ministries Inc. Lee's
Summit, MO

Jon Zens is one of few scholars enabled by the Holy Spirit to remove the tainted lenses of traditional interpretation in order to clearly see God's ways. This study of 1 Tim. 2 offers a broader panoramic view than any other book I have read. My heart leaps with excitement as I consider the freedom soon to be experienced and expressed by our brothers and sisters who will see new light in *What's with Paul & Women*? I truly believe the Lord was with Jon when he wrote this book!

—**Bonnie Jaeckle**, blogger, whole-heartedlife.
blogspot.com, Diagonal, IA

My endorsement of *What's with Paul and Women?* Does not come from a scholarly vantage point, but from a very personal one, straight from my heart. You see, I grew up in a denomination where women were very much subservient to men and were required to show their holiness by the way they looked and acted. The men, however, dressed in three-piece suits, slicked back their hair, wore two-tone shoes, could play sports and strutted around like cock roosters. I could not justify the discrepancies between the two. I queried often, "What do the men have to do to show their holiness?"

Jon Zens' book shows just how far back in church history such pervading attitudes have existed. He enlightens us to practices in many areas of the world where physical abuse and oppression of women still exist in the name of religion.

His research of Greek influence during New Testament times and his treatment of the Greek word, *hesuchia*, in I Timothy 2 provides a breath of fresh air concerning the role of women. That one nugget alone—that *hesuchia* means quietness, not silence—is worth the entire book. What a wonderful gift Jon has imparted to the questioning mind concerning the woman's role both as wife, as well as a fulfilled member of the body of Christ, with the same rights and privileges as men.

Many denominations in the past few centuries have permitted their noble women to go to foreign fields to preach the gospel. In fact, one major denomination named its missions organization after a woman. The church does not seem to have a problem with that particular role. We call them missionaries. As long as they are "over there," we tolerate their preaching to the masses, which includes men.

I am grateful for the expansion of this book which arches like a beautiful rainbow over the New Testament to encapsulate all the teachings regarding the functions of women, especially the marvelous redemptive role of Jesus to the women he encountered, which went against the grain of Jewish tradition.

> —**Rheba B. Drye**, B. S., East Carolina University,
> Pastor's wife at Harvest Cathedral,
> Macon, GA, 1978-2000

If you would like to contact Jon with questions or dialog about this book, write: jzens@searchingtogether.org or call him at either 715-338-2796 or 651-465-6516.

WHAT'S WITH PAUL AND WOMEN?

WHAT'S WITH PAUL AND WOMEN?
UNLOCKING THE CULTURAL BACKGROUND TO 1 TIMOTHY 2

JON ZENS

LINCOLN, NEBRASKA

WHAT'S WITH PAUL AND WOMEN?
UNLOCKING THE CULTURAL BACKGROUND TO 1 TIMOTHY 2
JON ZENS

LIBRARY OF CONGRESS CONTROL NUMBER: 2010924192

PUBLISHER'S CATALOGING-IN-PUBLICATION
(PROVIDED BY QUALITY BOOKS, INC.)

ZENS, JON.
  WHAT'S WITH PAUL AND WOMEN? : UNLOCKING THE CULTURAL
BACKGROUND TO 1 TIMOTHY 2 / BY JON ZENS.
  P. CM.
  INCLUDES BIBLIOGRAPHICAL REFERENCES.
  LCCN 2010924192
  ISBN-13: 978-0-9765222-9-4
  ISBN-10: 0-9765222-9-2

  1. BIBLE. N.T. TIMOTHY, 1ST, II--CRITICISM,
INTERPRETATION, ETC. 2. SEX ROLE--BIBLICAL TEACHING.
3. WOMEN IN THE BIBLE.   I. TITLE.

BS2745.6.S37Z46 2010   227'.8306
                              QBI10-600057

This volume is printed on acid free paper and meets ANSI Z39.48 standards.

Cover design by: Mark Sequeira, MJAStudios, Gilbert, AZ 2010

Printed in the United States of America

Ekklesia Press is a ministry to help authors get published and to publish works that are not deemed "profitable" by the mainstream publishing industry. Our goal is to put works into print that will impact and motivate followers of Christ to fulfill the Great Commission in an ever increasing way.

Ekklesia Press is an extension of www.kingdomcitizenship.org/wp

Author's Note: Throughout this book I have in many cases given my own translation of the Greek text. Otherwise, I have used the New International Version, NIV, Copyright 1973, 1978, 1984 by International Bible Society. Used by permission of Zondervan.

CONTENTS:

Dedication/Acknowledgements: **14**
Foreword by Wade Burleson: **15**
Introduction: **23**

1. How the New Testament Views Women   **27**
2. Two Preliminary "Why's?"   **33**
3. The Immediate Context of 1 Tim. 2   **35**
4. Why Paul Unites Modesty With Female Prayer   **39**
5. Quietness, Learning and Submission   **43**
6. Post-Apostolic Mistreatment of Women   **53**
7. Is Paul Concerned About Women Teaching?   **63**
8. Why Note That Adam Came First?   **73**
9. What About Eve Being Deceived?   **79**
10. The Gospel Applied to Cultural Situations   **83**
11. Conclusion & Summary   **87**

Appendix I — Regarding the Ephesian Social World   **91**
        [A Response by Dr. Frank R. Ames]
Appendix II — New Light on 1 Cor. 14:34-36   **97**
Appendix III — "In the Lord, however..." 1 Cor. 11:11 **107**
Sources for Further Study   **135**

DEDICATION:

*I am honored to dedicate this book to
Robert & Ida Scott*

—and—

*Dr. Robert & Lori Scott
whose Christ-centered love & sacrifice
have meant so much to Dotty & me*

ACKNOWLEDGEMENTS:

I would especially like to thank Wilma Bell, Joyce and Cliff Bjork, Annette Brians, Gordon Gillesby, Timothy L. Price and Mark Sequeira from the bottom of my heart for all their help in various ways as this project came to fruition. The first draft of this manuscript was written in March, 2007. Since then, it has been read by numerous people and I am thankful for the feedback that came from all of these folks. For sure, "in the abundance of counselors there is victory" (*cf.* Prov. 11:14; 24:6)!

FOREWORD:

In 2004 Dr. Sheri Klouda was terminated from her position as the distinguished professor of Hebrew at Southwestern Theological Seminary in Fort Worth, Texas. The seminary's new President and all male administration held to a belief that a Christian woman should never teach men, and so they released Dr. Klouda from the job of her dreams. Forced to relocate, Sheri took a far less prestigious faculty position at a Christian college in Indiana. Though bestowed a doctorate in Hebrew by Southwestern Seminary, she was removed from the very institution that trained her because the new men in charge followed what they perceived to be a biblical and theological principle that forbids women from teaching men (*cf.* 1 Tim. 2:12). When I discovered what happened to Sheri, I personally reached out to her family, knowing that the ideology that led to her firing was inconsistent with the teachings and ministry of Jesus Christ. Yet, at the time, I had few tools to argue against the errant interpretation of 1 Timothy 2:12.

Later that same year, during the last business session that I moderated as President of the Baptist General Convention of Oklahoma, an extraordinary, godly woman from a local metropolitan church was elected second vice-president of the convention. I will never forget the sight from the platform as several men throughout the auditorium stood and *literally turned their backs to the platform* as they voted "against" the first woman to be elected to general office within the BGCO. I was shocked at the rude behavior of my fellow pastors, for I knew them to be sincere, Bible-believing men. I later discovered that many of these brothers in Christ planned their visual protest out of the mistaken belief that our convention was violating 1 Timothy 2:12. Their ideology forbade them to allow any woman to "exercise authority" over men. Again, intuitively I knew that their actions reflected an incorrect understanding of Jesus' teachings regarding women, but I did not know how to respond to their dogmatic assertions of the meaning of this text.

A couple of years later, I received a written communication from a young lady in seminary, who confessed that she was writing to me with tears in her eyes. She had just come from her preaching class where the professor allowed all the men and boys in the class to remove themselves from the room so they would not be "subjected to hearing a woman teach the Word of God." The young lady found herself preaching to the walls and couldn't help but feel real isolation and shame. She asked me to help her reconcile the teaching of Paul in 1 Timothy 2:12 with the clear teachings of the rest of the New Testament regarding gender equality within the assembly. Her request, the two events described above, and other circumstances in my life since then, have created an awakening within me. I am committed to correct the warped, unbiblical view of women held by many Bible-believing, evangelical Christians; a view based on a wrong understanding of Paul's writings. Similar to 19th century evangelicals who believed the Bible condoned institutional slavery, some evangelicals pass their toxic view of women off as orthodox. For this to change, other Bible-believing Christians are going to have to show their brothers in Christ where they err in their interpretation of Paul's words in 1 Timothy 2.

Enter author Jon Zens. The book you hold in your hands is comparable to an antidote for a venomous snake bite. The viper known as "the doctrine of male authority" has bitten the church. The toxin emitted by this errant teaching affects the females within our assemblies. It debilitates their God-given gifts, denigrates their Spirit-led ministry, and downplays their role as New Covenant priests. Those of us who have seen the church bitten need assistance, and help has arrived. This book will help you suck out the venom of *male only* authority within the church. It will do so by helping you be able to articulate Jesus' view of the equality of women and then revealing for you how Paul's words in 1 Timothy 2 are consistent with Jesus' own teaching and ministry. You will be able to point out to others how the modern institutional church has misconstrued and misinterpreted Paul's writings on the subject, while at the same time ignoring Jesus' words and life on the same subject.

It is evident from Scripture that Jesus went about His public ministry with both males and females accompanying Him and ministering beside Him (*cf.* Luke 8:1-3). The New Testament gives many examples of women teaching men (*cf.* Luke 2:25-38; Acts 21:9; John 4:28-29). We are told in the Bible that women served as *deaconia* in the early church (*cf.* Rom. 16:1-2), and were co-laborers with men in the kingdom of Christ (*cf.* Rom. 16:3). At least one of the apostles was female (*cf.* Rom. 16:7). It's clear that Jesus' entire ministry on earth included gifted, ministering women (*cf.* John 4:28-29; John 20:1-2; Luke 24:1-11; Acts 1:14-15; Acts 2:17-18). The apostle Paul encouraged *both* men and women to teach, pray and participate fully in the assembly (*cf.* I Cor. 11:4-5 and I Cor. 14:23-24). Jesus' view of women and their place in the kingdom, echoed by the apostles, was a radical departure from the ancient Jewish understanding of female involvement, or lack thereof, in temple worship.

In Old Covenant days, those with spiritual *authority* were the elderly Jewish males who served as priests and leaders of covenant Israel. The Old Covenant had its laws, and obedience to them was essential for divine favor (*cf.* Exo. 19:5-8). But Jesus came to institute a new agreement, and He turned the concept of spiritual authority upside down. No longer would "authority" in the kingdom be based on gender, race or cultural status (*cf*. Gal. 3:28). Authority in the assembly would spring from the Holy Spirit who leads every New Covenant believer, both male and female, to be the "*servant of all*" (*cf*. Mark 9:35). For some modern Christians, it is difficult to see the radical nature of Jesus' teaching regarding the equality of women. There's a tendency for Christian males to fall back on the comfortable, ancient, societal and covenantal laws—whether it be ancient Israel's laws or old United States' laws—instead of embracing the freedom that comes through the teachings of Jesus Christ. But God won't let us rest in our view of women when it is similar to that of the ancients. He pushes us to listen to His Son.

When Jesus took Peter, James and John to the top of the mountain He was transfigured before their very eyes. The garments of Jesus turned blazing white. But what happened next was even more amazing. The great leaders of ancient Israel, Moses and Elijah, suddenly appeared and began conversing with Jesus. Peter, James and John watched all this happen in amazement. Becoming afraid, and not knowing what to do or say, Peter blurted out, "*Jesus, I think we should build some tents for you, Moses and Elijah, and we should stay up here and visit with all three of you. It's good for us to be here.*" Suddenly, a cloud descended around them, and God spoke to Peter, James and John in a clear and unequivocal voice. "*This is my beloved Son, hear him!*" (*cf*. Mark 9:7). The last two words are emphatic—*akouete auton*—**hear Him**! It's as if God is saying "Hear Him, not them!" The scripture says that as soon as God spoke, the disciples looked around and saw nobody with them—except Jesus alone (*cf.* Matt. 17:8). Jesus Christ is the apex of God's revelation to humans.

It's time that the body of Christ, the Christian church, listen again to Jesus when it comes to women. Some liberals argue that Paul's view of women was diametrically opposed to Jesus' views. They say the apostle was a misogynist, whose hatred of women caused him to tell them to "keep silent" in church and "be in subjection to men" (*cf.* 1 Tim. 2). In this book, Jon Zens corrects that inaccurate allegation against Paul by showing the apostle believed, just like Jesus, in the full equality of women with men. Zens brilliantly details how Paul's instruction to young Timothy—who himself was an assistant to the apostle in a city consumed by a belief in *female* superiority—proves that Paul understood that Jesus brings functional equality to women.

Unlike liberals, many conservative evangelical Christians believe Paul loved women, but he instructed them to be silent around men, to refrain from ever taking "spiritual authority," and to always be in subjection to male authority, because God designed women to be functionally subordinate to men. Zens, a conservative evangelical himself, shows how this conservative view of male authority is based on a misinterpretation of Paul's writings to Timothy, and is an outright denial of the gospels themselves. To silence women in the assembly, to prevent them from teaching men, to forbid them from sharing responsibilities with men, and to somehow say that a woman's place is to be subservient to men, is to deny the teaching and ministry of Jesus Christ as portrayed by the New Testament writers. It's almost as if we need another cloud to descend and have God to speak to us those clear words—Hear Him! The beauty and brilliance of *What's With Paul and Women?* is that it allows the reader to see, maybe for the first time, how Paul's instructions in 1 Timothy 2 are consistent with Jesus' belief in the full, functional equality of women within the assembly.

My prayer for you is that this vital book will set you free from the fear of being labeled a liberal, or a radical feminist, or a Christian who does not believe the Bible because of your belief in gender equality within the church. I pray that this book will enable you to identify the errant teachings of the institutional church regarding women, to gracefully resist those who seek to force silence upon gifted women, and to remain unaffected by the slanderous attacks of other conservative evangelicals who suggest that those of us who believe in gender equality do not believe the Bible. My prayer is that you will remain steadfast and true to your Lord and Savior Jesus Christ when it comes to your view of women. In short, I pray that you will "**hear Him!**" Jon Zens' book will help you do just that.

Wade Burleson
Emmanuel Baptist Church
http://kerussocharis.blogspot.com/
Enid, Oklahoma
April 2010

Artist's Rendering of Artemis

INTRODUCTION:

In 1709 the Vicar and Lecturer of Dedham in Essex, William Burkitt, offered these words of instruction from 1 Timothy 2:11-12:

> Still our Apostle is directing *Timothy* how persons should and ought to manage themselves in the Publick Assemblies, and particularly how Women ought to behave themselves at the Time and in the Place of Worship; let, says he, the Woman in your Assemblies *learn in silence with all subjection* to the better Sex; for I *suffer not a woman to teach* publickly, and to *usurp authority over the man*, to whom God has given Authority over her, but rather, according to her Duty, let her learn in Silence (*Expository Notes, with Practical Observations, on the New Testament of Our Lord & Saviour Jesus Christ*, 4ᵗʰ Edition, London, 1709, loc. cit.).

Learned British Baptist, John Gill, in the late 1700's gave his interpretation of 1 Timothy 2:11-12 with all confidence:

The apostle goes on to give some other instructions to women, how they should behave themselves in public worship, in the church of God; he would have them be learners and not teachers, sit and hear, and learn more of Christ...and he would have them learn in silence, and not offer to rise and speak, under a pretence of having a word from the Lord, or of being under an impulse of the Spirit of the Lord, as some frantic women have done.... They may teach in private, in their own houses and families...but then women are not to teach in the church; for that is an act of power and authority, and supposes the persons that teach be of a superior degree, and in a superior office, and to have superior abilities to those who are taught by them (*An Exposition of the Old & New Testaments*, 1853 [reprint, 1960], Vol. 6, pp. 599-600).

These two examples are illustrative of the fact that in the history of the church 1 Timothy 2:11-12 has been used unrelentingly as a proof-text to swiftly and decisively squelch the ministry of women in fellowships. Sadly, these are by no means isolated incidents nor has this trend decreased over time. More recently, in 1987, the assembly pastored by Nancy Sehested was put out of the Memphis Association of Southern Baptist Churches, and I Timothy 2:12 was a key component used in justifying this decision. In 2004, Sheri Klouda, a theology professor, was let go from her position at Southwestern Baptist Theological Seminary in Ft.

Worth, Texas, where she taught Hebrew. But the seminary leadership—based on 1 Timothy 2:12—concluded that a woman should not be "teaching men." *But is it really that simple?*

Carefully examining both Scriptural and historical contexts has brought me to question the traditional use of 1 Timothy 2:12 to silence female believers. If the "silence" use of I Timothy 2:12 rests on very questionable assumptions, then women in the body of Christ have been put under an unfounded bondage based on a serious misinterpretation of a critical Scriptural passage. Few would deny that 1 Timothy 2:11-15 is attended with difficulties at every level—contextual, cultural, linguistic, grammatical and conceptual. Nevertheless, for those truly desiring light from God's Word, sufficient truth can be uncovered showing that the traditional understanding of I Timothy 2:12 is riddled with dubious assumptions and even prejudices. If this is so, then in reality it has been used to abuse the female half of the Christian priesthood. The evidence is such that Bible teachers and church leaders would do well to reconsider this too common application of 2:11-15, which, in light of what follows in this book, appears to be misguided and unwarranted.

Jon Zens
March, 2010

If you would like to contact Jon with questions or dialog about this book, write: jzens@searchingtogether.org or call him at either 715-338-2796 or 651-465-6516.

(Woman) had never known
a man like this Man...
A prophet and teacher
Who never nagged at them...
Who never mapped out their
sphere for them,
never urged them
to be feminine
or jeered at them
for being female;
Who had no axe to grind
and no uneasy male dignity to
defend...

— D.L. Sayers

CHAPTER 1

HOW THE NEW TESTAMENT VIEWS WOMEN

Before we examine 1 Timothy 2:12 which, along with 1 Corinthians 14:34-35, has traditionally been used to restrict believing women, it is imperative that we review the overwhelmingly positive picture of Abraham's daughters painted for us in the New Testament (cf. Luke 13:16). These many passages should not be simply dismissed or forgotten when considering the two "problem" texts.

Neither the Gospel narratives nor the recorded words of Jesus *ever* put restrictions on the ministry of women.

Jesus fully and completely accepted women as his disciples and they accompanied him in his travels with the male disciples (*cf.* Luke 8:1-3). These women also supported the mission of Jesus with their own resources. These facts are much more significant than they might initially appear. In first century Jewish culture it was unheard of for a Jewish rabbi to have or want female followers. Luke reports this rather matter-of-factly; yet this band of women and men who accompanied Jesus as they went from place to place would hardly seem kosher to the curious Jewish onlookers.

After Simeon took the baby Jesus in his arms and saw God's salvation, Anna the prophetess "gave thanks to God and spoke of Him [Jesus] to all the ones expecting redemption in Jerusalem" (*cf.* Luke 2:25-38). Anna did not just proclaim Christ to women, but to "all."

Jesus applauded the evangelistic efforts of the Samaritan woman (*cf.* John 4:35-38). After experiencing a revelation of Jesus, she left her jar at the well and went to her city telling men, women and children about the Messiah (*cf.* John 4:28-29). Everyone in Sychar knew about her history of broken relationships, yet she boldly proclaimed Jesus as the Messiah—a Redeemer even for those outside of Judaism!

In the context of Jesus' crucifixion the male disciples fled, yet the women stayed with him and helped with his burial (*cf.* Matt. 27:55-56, 61; Mark 15:40-41; Luke 23:55-56; John 19:25-27).

A woman's testimony was disallowed as evidence in first century courts. Yet the Lord chose females to be the first witnesses and lead the proclamation of his resurrection (*cf.* John 20:1-2, 11-18; Luke 24:1-11, 22-24; Mark 16:1-8; Matt. 28:1-11).

After Christ's ascension, 120 men *and women* prayed together and chose a replacement for Judas Iscariot (*cf.* Acts 1:14-15).

The Spirit came upon the 120 disciples and they all spoke the wonderful works of God in many foreign languages (*cf.* Acts 2:1-4).

Some thought that what occurred on the Day of Pentecost was evidence of too much wine, but Peter insisted that it was a fulfillment of what Joel prophesied would come to pass—"your sons and daughters will prophesy.... I will pour out my Spirit on my male and female slaves and they will prophesy" (*cf.* Acts 2:17-18). There is nothing to suggest that males alone were allowed to prophesy freely, while the females were restricted in some ways.

Philip the evangelist had four virgin daughters who prophesied (*cf.* Acts 21:9). Since there is no cause to believe these daughters were somehow exceptional or rare, we are justified in assuming that there were many other sisters who had this gift, not just Philip's offspring.

Paul entrusted his letter to the Romans to Phoebe who delivered it for him. She was a deacon in the assembly at Cenchrea and Paul held her in the highest regard (*cf.* Rom. 16:1-2). Paul recognized her as a *prostatis*, a Greek word which carries with it the idea of leadership (*cf.* 1 Thes. 5:12).

Paul designated Priscilla and Aquila as his "co-workers" (cf. Rom. 16:3). The same word, *sunergos*, is used with reference to people like Timothy and Titus.

Junia and Andronicus [wife/husband or sister/brother] were greeted by Paul as "outstanding among the apostles" (cf. Rom. 16:7). They were his relatives and had been in prison with him. Clearly, there were many identified as "apostles," like Barnabas, who were not among the original Twelve. Junia was also among such apostolic workers. There is no reason to think that she was the only such female apostle or that female apostles were regarded as rare or unusual. This illustrates that apostolic labor was not male-specific.

Among all the people Paul greeted in Romans 16, ten were sisters among whom were "Tryphena and Tryphosa [who may have been twins], women who work hard for the Lord" (cf. Rom. 16:12).

In line with Acts 2:17-18, Paul encouraged brothers and sisters to prophesy in the gatherings (cf. 1 Cor. 11:4-5; 14:23-24).

The open meeting Paul described in 1 Corinthians 14 envisioned all the men and women—"the whole assembly"—"each one of you"—"you may all prophesy one by one"—functioning together in an encouraging manner.

Galatians 3:28 indicates that "in Christ" human

distinctions, like male and female, are no longer norms of judgment in the congregation. In the first century, prejudices abounded in folks' minds when certain people like "Gentile," "Jew," "slave," and "woman" were mentioned. Paul stated that in the body of Christ this should not be the case. The implication is one that is not limited to formal gatherings of Christians, but is a standard means of relating to others in all contexts.

Women were prominent in the assembly at Philippi, beginning with Lydia's home. In Philippians 4:2-3 Paul asked for two sisters—who must have had no small spiritual influence in the body—to be at peace with one another. He called Euodia and Syntyche "co-workers" and "co-strugglers" in the gospel.

2 John is addressed to "the elect lady and her children." This probably referred to a respected sister in whose home the saints gathered. She apparently exerted significant spiritual influence upon a number of people. Women's homes were mentioned as meeting places for the brethren in Romans 16:5, 1 Corinthians 1:11, 16:19 and Colossians 4:15.

In Revelation 2:20-24 Christ rebuked the Thyatiran congregation for allowing a false prophetess, nicknamed "Jezebel," to "teach" some of the Lord's servants to sin grievously. If it was such a crime for a woman to teach the brethren, why didn't the Lord just condemn the assembly for even allowing a woman to instruct others? This incident in Thyatira implies that the assembly permitted other male and female prophets to teach the truth. Christ's objection was not that *a woman taught*, but that *what she taught* was false teaching. We will come back to this passage in the course of our investigation of 1 Timothy 2:12.

This vital survey of New Testament highlights concerning women reveals the freedom of the sisters to function in the kingdom. The general flow of the New Testament reveals no need for females to walk on eggshells because of any alleged "restrictions" put upon them by the Lord. Such a survey should also serve as a corrective to those who suppress and intimidate women by using their interpretation of two passages —1 Corinthians 14:34-35 and 1 Timothy 2:12— as a means to cancel out the obvious ministry of sisters unfolded in other Scriptures.

I believe the information we have in the Bible about women is most significant for another reason. *Have you ever thought about the fact that we have in the New Testament more glimpses into the service of women in the Kingdom than we do concerning most of the twelve apostles?* The Lord has given us more information about the functioning of sisters than he has about a lot of other people, places and matters that typically pique our curiosity!

TWO PRELIMINARY "WHY'S?"

Why Are 1 & 2 Timothy and Titus Called "Pastoral" Epistles? Before coming to our passage in 1 Timothy, it is vital to note that the tradition of designating 1 & 2 Timothy and Titus as "Pastoral" Epistles is very misleading. One writer calls Timothy a "young pastor."[1] This reveals a mistaken assumption because clearly Timothy and Titus were *not* resident pastors/elders. They were itinerant apostolic assistants. Paul "left" them in various places to help the assemblies. Paul at one point told Timothy to "do the work of an evangelist" (*cf.* 2 Tim. 4:5). In these three letters Paul gave his co-workers instructions regarding issues and problems faced by the assemblies they moved among and assisted. As Frank Viola rightly observes:

> Labeling 1 Timothy, 2 Timothy and Titus the "Pastoral Epistles" or the "Pastorals" is a misnomer. These letters were not given this label until the 18th century. Timothy and Titus were not pastors. They were apostolic workers.[2]

Why Was 1 Timothy Written? The primary purpose of 1 Timothy is stated by Paul in 1:3-4 — "As I urged you upon my departure to Macedonia, remain on at Ephesus, in order that you may instruct certain persons to neither teach differently, nor to pay attention to myths and unending genealogies, which stir up questions rather than furthering the steward- ship of God in faith." "The key to understanding the letter," Gordon Fee notes, "lies in taking seriously that Paul's stated reason in (*cf.* 1:3) for leaving Timothy in Ephesus is the real one; namely, that he has been left there to combat some false teachers, whose asceticism and speculative nonsense based on the law are engendering strife, causing many to capitulate to the false teaching."[3] William M. Ramsay concurs that "the charge imposed on Timothy (*cf.* 1:3) is the guiding thought of the whole letter."[4]

1 Timothy is not a universal church manual for a pastor. It is a mandate for an apostolic assistant to deal with serious issues involving false teaching in Ephesus. Unfortunately, some women had apparently become involved in this problem.

Endnotes:
[1] David P. Kuske, "Exegesis of 1 Timothy 2:11-15," at www.wisessays.net/authors/k/kusketimothy
[2] Frank Viola, *The Untold Story of the New Testament Church*, Destiny Image, 2004, p. 160.
[3] Gordon Fee, *Gospel & Spirit: Issues in New Testament Hermeneutics*, Hendrickson, 1991, p. 54.
[4] *Historical Commentary on the Pastoral Epistles*, edited by Mark Wilson, Kregel, 1996, p. 11.

CHAPTER 3

THE IMMEDIATE CONTEXT OF 1 TIM. 2

In terms of the basic structure Paul used in this chapter we can observe the following [I have noted the singular and plural subjects in 2:1-15]:

- "I *exhort* [the whole assembly to pray]...to the end that we might live a peaceful and *quiet* life" (vv. 1-2).

- "I *will* that the males [plural] pray..." (v. 8).

- "Similarly [I will that] the women [plural] *pray* in proper clothing..." (v. 9).

- "Let a woman [singular] learn in quietness..." (v. 11).

- "But I am not now permitting a woman [singular] to teach with the goal of dominating a man [singular], but to be in quietness" (v. 12).

- "For Adam [singular] was first formed, then

Eve [singular]" (v. 13).

• "But she [singular] will be delivered through childbearing if they [plural] remain in faith" (v. 15).

The same Greek word, *hesuchia* [quietness], is used in verse 2 with reference to all believers leading a quiet life, in verse 11 with reference to a woman learning in quietness and in verse 12 with reference to a woman being in quietness. The word simply does not mean "silent." Verse 2 obviously does not envision us leading a "silent" life, but rather a life in which we are not known as contentious people. Thus any Bible version that has the woman in "silence" (*cf.* Tim. 2:11-12) reveals some level of bias, is a very inaccurate translation and leaves an impression upon the mind that is not from the Lord.

In the Ephesian congregation there were people promoting false teaching and, as a result, there was some disorder taking place. One can appreciate, then, why Paul would emphasize prayer among the brethren and then elaborate on the world-wide salvation purpose of God in Christ (vv. 3-7).

Philip H. Towner provides a crisp summary of the Ephesian church in the midst of its surrounding culture:

Ephesus was famed for its cult and temple

dedicated to the worship of Artemis, around which a good deal of the city's commercial interests revolved. It also had a large Jewish colony. Ephesus presented the gospel with a formidable challenge in that it was a center of pagan worship. From its inception here (*cf.* Acts 19) the church was very much in the public eye. When we speak of "the church" in Ephesus, we should understand a system [more or less] of house churches (*cf.* 1 Cor. 16:19).[5]

The implicit contrast between prayers in Christian assemblies and those in Jewish synagogues must also be underscored. Jews in the first century were under Roman rule. Their synagogue prayers focused on the destruction of their Gentile enemies, not their salvation. Paul, on the other hand, exhorts the assembly to intercede on behalf of those in civil power and for the salvation of people all over the world.

Endnotes:
[5] *1-2 Timothy & Titus,* The IVP New Testament Commentary Series, 1994, p. 21.

Artist's Rendition of Artemis Temple Activity

CHAPTER 4

WHY PAUL UNITES MODESTY WITH FEMALE PRAYER

"Similarly [I will that] the women [pray] in proper clothing. . . ."

"Both Acts 19 and the apocryphal *Acts of John* tell of the continuous conflict between the Christians at Ephesus and those who followed the religion of Artemis." —L.M. McDonald [6]

Some Christian denominations have used 1 Timothy 2:9 to teach that godly women must not wear jewelry, braid their hair, or wear lipstick —with no concern for the cultural background that led Paul to address this often misunderstood subject. Crucial light is shed upon his words once the pervasive influence that the goddess Artemis of Ephesus had in this 1st century city is factored in. Perhaps it could be likened to the influence that having the stronghold of Mormonism in Salt Lake City, Utah, has on local culture. The Temple of Artemis in Ephesus was a massive 98,000 square foot structure, and was one of the "seven wonders" of the world at that time.

Most importantly, the Temple operations were the driving economic force in Ephesus, drawing hundreds of thousands of people into the city annually. As in a modern city dependent upon one employer, almost everyone residing in this city probably drew their livelihood directly or indirectly from the Temple, the goddess Artemis and the cult surrounding her. Clearly, then, the new followers of Christ would be swimming against a very, very strong stream of local disfavor. This, I think, helps explain much of Paul's concern with dress and deportment among believing women, particularly when contrasted with the sexually-charged displays taking place in and around the Temple of Artemis.

Among other things, Artemis, a goddess within the Greek Pantheon, was the goddess of fertility and protection during childbirth, and had been worshipped at the Temple in Ephesus for at least 300 years prior to Paul's visit to Ephesus. So how did female Artemis-devotees in Ephesus seek her favor in prayer? "They offered supplications and thanksgiving by donning and presenting expensive attire and ornate hair."[7] Heliodorus [3rd century A.D.] noted: "The Artemisian supplicant makes prayers in crowns of olive branches. They do not sacrifice animals to [Artemis] because their locks of hair carry prayers (*Aeth.* 1.12)."[8]

In verse 8 Paul "desired" that men pray without

wrath and doubting. "Similarly," in verse 9 Paul desires that women pray—not with gaudy clothing, jewelry and fancy hair-dos—but in proper outward attire befitting godly women.

This instruction parallels 1 Corinthians 11:4-5 in the sense that Paul assumes that both men and women will be praying and prophesying in the gatherings of the saints. As renowned scholar William M. Ramsay put it, "it was customary for any of the brethren to speak in the assembled congregation as the Spirit moved them, both men and women."[9]

Endnotes:
[6] "Ephesus," *Dictionary of New Testament Background*, Craig A. Evans & Stanley E. Porter, eds., IVP, 2000, p. 321.
[7] Frank R. Ames, "Modest Dress, Public Silence, and Safety in Childbearing: Interpreting Paul's Instructions in 1 Timothy in Light of Ephesian Inscriptions, Artifacts and Traditions," presented at the International CBE Conference, Denver, CO, August 11, 2007, p. 15.
[8] Ibid., p. 16.
[9] *Historical Commentary on the Pastoral Epistles*, edited by Mark Wilson, Kregel, 1994, p. 32.

In [mankind's] sinful human
condition...man exploits...
woman's natural proclivity...
and subjugate[s] her.
Subjugation of woman,
in fact, is a symptom
of man's fallen nature.
If the work of Christ involves...
breaking...the fall,"
the implication of His work
for the liberation of women is
plain.

—F. F. Bruce

CHAPTER 5

QUIETNESS, LEARNING AND SUBMISSION

In trying to unravel these challenging texts, I am truly a debtor to the very hard work of many listed in the "Suggested Sources." Along with some possible insights that I have come to see, in most cases I am just calling attention to some foundational points others have unearthed through diligent research. I am going to structure my comments by contrasting the *traditional view* with some *correctives* warranted by textual, contextual and cultural considerations.

I appeal to you to follow my presentation with an open heart and a willingness to consider the evidence unfolded. There are many assumptions and layers of tradition that must be carefully evaluated. As John R.W. Stott has said, "To me the essence of being a radical is being willing to subject one's inherited traditions and conventions to biblical scrutiny."[10] "It may be that much of what we call *Christian*," notes Bill White, "would have to be thrown out in the light of Biblical re-education.... Let's approach Scripture with an open mind and heart and discover what God has called us to in the way of re-education and renewal."[11] Let's face it—we all struggle to let go of old things learned in order to give way to new things the Sprit unveils.

1 Timothy 2:11—"Let a woman learn in quietness in all submission"

TRADITIONAL VIEW:

The word *hesuchia* in many translations has been rendered as "silence," and many church leaders have taken this to mean that women are not to speak in church meetings. "All submission" is taken to mean that females are to be passive receivers, not active participants.

CORRECTIVES:

Hesuchia means "quietness," not "silence." Further, in 1 Timothy 2:2 the stated goal is for all believers to live a "quiet" life. In 1 Thessalonians 4:11 Paul instructs all the brethren, "strive eagerly to be quiet, to do your own business and work with your own hands." The apostle tells those believers who are not working "to work with quietness and to eat their own bread" (*cf.* 2 Thess. 3:12).

Since "quietness" is to be a quality of all the saints, if Paul mentions that a woman needs to learn in quietness, wouldn't that imply some special circumstance that required this instruction? Would this not also imply that it would be a serious mistake to create a universal prohibition from what is clearly directed to a specific problem? Is it not clear from the very same context that the males needed a dose of quietness too, as they were manifesting "wrath" among themselves and, presumably, towards others (v. 8)?

The fact that *hesuchia* does not mean "silence" illustrates the careless and wholly inappropriate use of Scripture by those who with arrogance and dogmatism cite 1 Timothy 2:12 as if it obviously puts an end to any further debate. Let's look at two examples of such misuse, one by a "clergy" person and another by a "lay" person.

1. In 1970, British Reformed theologian Donald MacLeod pontificated, "[In 1 Timothy 2:11-14] the woman is explicitly forbidden to aspire to the offices of teaching and ruling. She is to be submissive; she is to be a learner; she is to be silent. Paul does not qualify this last injunction in any way.... The injunction to silence, then, is comprehensive. Women are not to teach nor to rule nor to lead the public prayers of the congregation."[12] MacLeod's intimidating remarks are premised on the mistaken, to say the very least, claim that *hesuchia* means "silence." Everything he says here is built on this false foundation. He knows Greek very well and he should have known better, but he gives no evidence of caring what *hesuchia* really means in verses 2, 11 and 12. It certainly strongly suggests that the incorrect translation of the verses suited his authoritarian agenda, so he squeezed it for all it was worth.

2. In a letter to an editor, "Brother Richard" was so upset at "Liberals" for pointing out the presence of a female apostle in Romans 16:7 that he lashed out with what he clearly felt were the final words on the matter: "These liberals obviously do not accept the Reformation proclamation 'Scripture alone,' long a basic tenet of the Lutheran faith. You do not have to strain your brain to understand 1 Timothy 2:12, which states unequivocally, 'I do not permit a woman to teach or have authority over a man; she must be silent.' Delete this or any other sentence out of the Bible and you are now free to say or do anything you wish. '*Sola Scriptura!*'"[13]

It is not being unfair to state that very nearly all that breeds such dogmatism, especially in these cited cases, clearly is based on:

• Faulty translations of verses 11 and 12

• Hearing Bible teachers like MacLeod perpetuate false teaching about these verses

I am compelled to ask: isn't using Scripture like this exactly how cults take verses out of context to build false teaching upon them? For example, some cults assert that Christ is "only human" by citing a verse like "the Father is greater than I [Jesus]." But this totally disregards all the other biblical contexts that confirm His deity.

Scripture must be viewed and considered as a whole and within a context. Using any single Scripture to cancel out the combined impact of many Scriptures is, to say it in the kindest way possible, not a safe way to handle God's Word. Those who use 1 Timothy 2:12 as a proof-text to shut down women's ministry are guilty of using one Scripture to cancel out the clear and compelling biblical revelation of women ministering in *many* other settings. This misuse of 1 Timothy 2:11-12 is even more aggravating because these ill-informed "teachers" go on to impose a demeaning and frustrating "silence" on women when the Greek word, *hesuchia*, had no such meaning in the first place.

The way Mr. MacLeod and "Brother Richard" used 1 Timothy 2:11-12 also highlights another problem that must be squarely faced. Too many people-in-the-pews read their chosen Bible translation assuming it is completely accurate and trustworthy. Leland Ryken rightly observes:

> *Readers who do not know the original biblical languages assume that an English translation reproduces what the Bible really says....* People naturally and legitimately appeal to the English translation in their hands as constituting "what the Bible says"....

Readers of the English translation operate on the premise that they are reading what the Bible actually says.[14]

I shudder to think of all the times in the past 500 years that church leaders have publicly employed an English translation of 1 Timothy 2:11-12 to silence women, as if these verses were the last and final words on the matter. But they were mistaken. All the older pulpit translations had wrongly translated *hesuchia* as "silence." How many times have Bible teachers confidently asserted, "The silence of women is stated right here in God's Word as clear as a bell. You can read it; I can read it. Therefore, we are constrained to obey this injunction." But the translation before them is actually erroneous, and as a result untold damage is being done to the body of Christ. *There is absolutely nothing illegitimate about researching to better comprehend —even to confirm or deny— that a particular translation is correct.*

"In all submission." Again, the New Testament clearly teaches that "submission" is to be an attribute of all believers, not just the sisters (*cf.* the further discussion of Ephesians 5:21-32 in my review article of John Piper's *What's the Difference?* in Appendix Three).

Romans 13:1, 5 – every person is to be subject to the civil authorities.

1 Corinthians 14:32 – the spirits of the prophets

are subject to [under the self-control of] the prophets.

1 Corinthians 16:15, 16 — the brethren are to submit to those who lay down their lives for others.

Ephesians 5:21 — all Christians are to mutually submit to one another in the fear of Christ.

James 4:7 — we are all to submit to the Lord.

1 Peter 5:5 — all of you, be subject one to another.

We must ask, do only women learn in all submission? Do men somehow learn in a different way, without submission? Are not "quietness" and "submission" necessary qualities in order for *anyone* to learn? If this is indeed the case, then surely we are warranted in suggesting that there must have been a problem with some subset of women, or a particular woman, which fully accounts for why Paul would issue this *special* directive.

"*Let a woman learn* [Greek, *manthano*]..." We must not forget that learning in apostolic times was not male-driven and certainly not pulpit-centered. It was a body experience in which *all* participated. We have already seen that both men and women are free to prophesy (*cf.* Acts 2:17-18; 1 Cor. 11:3-5). Paul made it crystal clear in 1 Corinthians14 that he wanted prophecy from both genders to be central in the gathering. In 1 Corinthians 14:31 he directs the saints in this manner: "you may all [males and females] prophesy one by one, so that all [men and women] may learn [*manthano*] and all may be encouraged." In the New Testament even singing results in teaching and admonishing (*cf.* Eph. 5:19; Col. 3:16).

Nowhere in the New Testament are sisters forbidden to contribute to the learning process according to their gifts and graces. Thus, Paul's concern as expressed in 1 Timothy 2:11-12 *must have* been rooted in problems that surfaced within the Ephesian congregation. Some women, or a woman, were involved in giving or propagating false teachings and were therefore admonished to be in a learning posture at that time. It only makes sense that generally speaking the assembly benefits and thrives from the input of both brothers and sisters. Donald Joy makes this astute observation:

> We are always impoverished when a single sex group meets, discusses, and makes decisions, since only part of the full-spectrum personhood seems to be present. So where urgent decisions are being made, we surely want both sexes speaking and voting.[15]

It is noteworthy that from a practical standpoint the traditional "male headship/female submission"

notion has been one of the most abused concepts
in the flow of church history. In the past and in the
present it is very easy for males with controlling spirits
to use "male headship" as a "Biblical" justification to
keep women under their thumbs.

In my personal journey I have seen repeatedly the
importance of sorting out what the New Testament
actually teaches, versus the traditions that have been
added on, or the negative influence of baggage that we
read into texts. Let's apply these realities to the topic
of marriage. It cannot be denied that the NT connects
certain words with the marriage relationship. But did
the NT mean by those words the same things that were
connected to them by post-apostolic theologians? For
example, and all too commonly, many assume that
"male headship" means that the husband has "authority
over" the wife, and not a few assume it means that *all
women* are to be subject to *all men.*

Practicing the New Testament perspectives on
marriage—oneness, equality, husband as "head," the
wife as "submissive"—are tricky, especially when
factoring in the peculiar chemistry of personalities
that each couple brings to the table. When Paul
mentions "in all submission" in 1 Timothy 2 it does
not appear that the marriage relationship is in his
immediate consideration. His probable intent was
rather submission to gospel teaching.

When the apostle mentions the wives' submission

in Ephesians 5:22, the intimate connection of this verse with verse 21 is noteworthy. In verse 21 the last of five participles—"submitting"—that flow out of a Spirit-filled life is given. *Mutual submission to one another in the body of Christ is an outgrowth of Spirit-fullness.* In verse 22 there is no verb—"The wives to their own husbands...." The verb must be drawn from verse 21 —"The wives to their own husbands [submit]...." In Ephesians 5:22-33 the husband being the "head" has nothing to do with "authority over" the wife. Most of the instruction in this passage is directed toward the husbands, who are to nourish, cherish and lay down their lives for their brides. In the gospel age the husband-wife relationship is to be a reflection of how Christ and the church relate. The benchmark is not the sin-based gender war of Genesis 3:16, but the gospel-bathed "symphony" of husband and wife working together under Christ's Lordship (*cf.* 1 Cor. 7:5).

FURTHER REFLECTION:

Great sources on marriage, headship and submission can be found in Patricia Gundry, *Heirs Together: Mutual Submission in Marriage* (Zondervan, 1980, 192pp.); John C. Howell, *Equality & Submission in Marriage* (Broadman, 1979, 140pp.); and I. Howard Marshall, "Mutual Love & Submission in Marriage, Col. 3:18-19 & Eph. 5:21-33," *Discovering Biblical Equality*, Pierce & Groothuis, eds. (IVP, 2005), pp. 186-204.

Endnotes:

[10] *Evangelical Newsletter*, April 30, 1982, p. 3.

[11] *Searching Together*, Spring, 1983, p. 32.

[12] "The Place of Women in the Church," *Banner of Truth*, #81, June, 1970, p. 3.

[13] *Christian News*, March 26, 2007, p. 19.

[14] *The Word of God in English: Criteria for Excellence in Bible Translation*, Crossway Books, 2002, p. 136.

[15] *Bonding: Relationships in the Image of God*, 2nd ed., Evangel, 1999, p. 25.

CHAPTER 6

POST-APOSTOLIC MISTREATMENT OF WOMEN

The retrogression that occurred with reference to women in the post-apostolic age can be compared to what happened in other doctrinal and practical areas. For example, the Lord's Supper was transformed from a time of the brethren remembering the Lord in a meal together to an elaborate "Holy Sacrament" officiated over by a clergyman.[16] The monumental difference, however, between such things as the Lord's Supper and what happened to women was that half of the church was rendered inferior and marginalized for nearly two millennia.

The too-common assumption that "male head-ship" means "authority over" and then connecting it to all decision-making is a post-enlightenment, science-based understanding which came into being when the role of the anatomical brain was identified. That perception has only been common for the last several hundred years. But in the first century it was the "heart" [or even the stomach], not the "head" that was believed to be the seat of decision-making, and there is much varied evidence to suggest that "authority over" would not have generally been connected to the concept of "head" in the cultures of Paul's day.[17]

Again, many assume that male headship must result in the virtual non-expression of the wife's gifts. However, Scripture does nothing whatever to confirm such a lop-sided notion. Both Huldah and Deborah were functioning prophetesses, but that did not keep them from being godly wives, as their husbands' names are mentioned. The *ekklesia* submits to her Husband, but Christ's purpose is not to silence his people, but to see all of the gifts in his Bride blossom and come to full expression.

Most people are glaringly ignorant of a vastly significant historical reality. Paul indeed used the words "head" and "submission" with reference to husbands and wives. There is, however, a huge chasm between what Paul likely had in mind with those words and how they were subsequently misappropriated and merged into the "mind-body dualism of classical Greek philosophy" by the early church fathers in order to elevate their own authority while utterly suppressing women in home and church.[18] From within the then reigning viewpoint of Greek philosophy, males were assumed to be connected with the superior "mind" [spirituality] while females were connected with the assumed inferior "body" [carnal lust]. Thus Origen "taught that women are more closely connected to the flesh than men and thus not as spiritual," and Augustine "associates women with the evil flesh that must be controlled by the spirit, which he believed was superior in men."[19] Thus the "goal of salvation was to free the pure soul from the evil material body."[20] The state of celibacy became exalted upon the basis of this "Platonic spirituality" which exalted the unseen realms and denigrated the body. The most spiritual posture, it was presumed increasingly by the church, was to separate oneself from all sexual expression. Translated into daily life this meant, "keep away from women, for they are the gateway into lust and profligacy,"[21] which was, of course, not true then or now.

> Women are thereby assimilated into the very definition of sin. The bodily principle is seen [in Philo and the Church Fathers] as so intrinsic-ally demonic that the high road to salvation demands the spurning of bodily life altogether for the ascetical virgin state. Sexuality and procreation correspond to the lower realm of corruption…the carnal realm was regarded as female…the female, even as a nun, [is regarded] as the dangerous embodiment of the "fleshly principle."[22]

Flowing from this, female sexuality came to be viewed as "responsible for the Fall of creation and the descent of man's soul into perdition."[23] Viewing women with disdain as the conduits for sin led of necessity to their subordination to males. "Since femaleness was equated with the inferior body, it followed that woman must naturally live in submission to man in hierarchical fashion, even as the body must be subject to the spirit."[24]

This degradation of females led not a few theologians to question whether women as entities separate from men were in God's image. Further, since women were seen as "lower beings," husbands were granted the right to correct or chastise their wives. This "gave religious and legal sanction for the absolute control of the 'male mind' over the 'female body,' in the form of physical violence."[25] Thus a perverted theology led to the church's sanctioning of wife-beating. The Council of Toledo in A.D. 400 "decreed that [clergy] had the right to beat their wives more severely than ordinary fellows: 'A husband is bound to chastise his wife moderately, unless he be a [clergy], in which case he may chastise her harder.' A later passage states that 'if wives of clergy transgress their [husbands'] commands, they may beat them, keep them bound in their house and force them to fast but not unto death.'"[26]

This helps us understand why church leaders were so uncaring when it came to the harsh treatment of women. John Calvin's letter to the wife of an abusive husband reflects the hardness of heart and utter insensitivity to the plight of women when he replied in part:

We have a special sympathy for women who are evilly and roughly treated by their husbands.… We do not find ourselves permitted by the Word of God, however, to advise a woman to leave her husband, except by force of necessity; and we do not find this force to be operative when a husband behaves roughly and uses threats to his wife, not even when he beats her, but only when there is imminent peril to her life.… We exhort her to bear with patience the cross which God has seen fit to place upon her; and meanwhile not to deviate from the duty which she has before God to please her husband, but to be faithful whatever happens.[27]

This vile outlook on women was already engrained in the theology of the Roman Catholic Church, and is amply documented in Uta Ranke-Heinemann's *Eunuchs for the Kingdom of Heaven: Women, Sexuality, & the Catholic Church* (Doubleday, 1990, 360pp.). It is imperative to keep in mind that the very essence of the assumptions about women in traditional theology are extremely suspect, to say the least. To link Paul's conceptions of "head" and "submission" with what is articulated in Tertullian, Augustine, Jerome and many other church fathers about females is a total abomination and a complete disconnect from the New Testament. There is no continuity of Paul's teaching with the later philosophic, anti-body pseudo-theology that came to dominate the visible church's practice.

Such a disconnect is strikingly illustrated when Donald MacLeod simplistically linked the views of women embedded in church history with New Testament statements. "Until comparatively recently there was virtually unanimous agreement among Christians that women should be excluded from the ordained ministries of the church.... The traditional practice of the Church can claim the explicit support of several New Testament passages."[28] MacLeod's last sentence is wrong, misleading and dangerous. As we have just seen, "the traditional practice of the Church" viewed women as inferior beings —conduits of the devil—who must be kept in line by a male hierarchy. Physical violence toward women was thus sanctioned by the church. This awful oppression of females was based on humanistic philosophy, not concern for biblical accuracy. Such diminution of women absolutely cannot claim the explicit or implicit support of any New Testament writings. What the New Testament said about sisters and what post-apostolic theologians said about women are two entirely different worlds. Further, church tradition held that *all women must be subject to all men.* The New Testament has *only* the marriage relationship in view when it speaks of "head" and "submission."

At a meeting in the Wesleyan Chapel in July, 1848, in Seneca Falls, New York, a Declaration of Sentiments on behalf of women noted that "in the covenant of marriage, she is compelled to promise obedience to her husband, he becoming, to all intents and purposes, her master—the law giving him power to deprive her of her liberty and to administer chastisement."[29] Again, we see that the physical "chastisement" of a wife was built into assumptions about marriage and protected by the law.

Can we begin to comprehend why most wives [women] in the world cringe when they hear about wifely [female] "submission" from the lips of church leadership? Ana Audilia Moreira de Campos in 1979 described the daily life of rural women in El Salvador. This same basic picture is sadly duplicated in most places around the world today.

> Men who earn little or no income have almost nothing to be proud of except their virility. They have few ways to relieve their frustrations, so women often bear the brunt of their discontents. There is absolutely no respect for the human dignity of women. It is common for their husbands and fathers to beat, kick and humiliate them in the most vulgar ways... . The majority of men in our rural communities refer to women as "idiots," "pigs," "worthless," "disobedient," "deceitful," "disloyal," "lazy," "stupid," and "daughters of whores"... . If it suits his mood, any of the above perceived qualities serve as sufficien t reason for him to mistreat his wife... . From the day she is born, a female is regarded as

inferior. The birth of a girl child is a great disappointment... . No one celebrates the birth of a girl... . The woman's job never ends. She has to work at least sixteen hours a day to complete her chores... . Men, however, think women's work has little value... . Women have become the nation's beasts of burden, shouldering the basic responsibilities of the family and society in order that men may be free to pursue whatever work and pleasures they desire... . The myth of women's inferiority continues to flourish because of traditional customs and educational biases that have conditioned both sexes to believe the male is superior... . This national inferiority has been created and forced by men. Institutionally, it is maintained and reinforced by the school system, the government, the Church, the community and the family.[30]

Notice that last sentence. National female inferiority "is maintained and reinforced by...the Church." How can we be surprised at this in light of the way women were treated in the history of the church? The church has led the way in suppressing women. What Paul meant by "submission" has nothing to do with the meaning it took on as the Greek philosophic body/soul notions infiltrated Christian theology.

In his *The Subversion of Christianity*, Jacques Ellul notes that when the church became powerful:

All that represented weakness or inferiority [physical, social, etc.] was put in second place. Women are the most spectacular instance of this. After a period of independence that came with the spread of Christianity, they were relegated to a lower order…[T]he more feminine liberty was suppressed, the more women were accused (of being the temptress of Genesis, etc.), [and] the more they were reduced to silence.[31]

This bottom-rung status of women in the post-apostolic age did not emerge because of careful study of Scripture. It came about as a result of the conflation of alien political and philosophical forces used by fallen men. "What began as a movement that offered dignity and equality to women," Ross Saunders observes, "ended up as an organization that was almost totally androcentric."[32] Thus, the second-century world of Tertullian was not really any different from most cultures in the 21st century world—"In our society, men control almost every facet of life. From the government to the Church, from political parties and cooperatives to sports, men run things."[33]

Endnotes:
[16] P.E. Kretzmann, "The Eucharist Between 30 and 325 A.D.," *Concordia Theological Monthly*, 1:3, 1930, pp. 167-183; Emil Brunner, *The Misunderstanding of the Church*, Lutterworth Press, 1954, pp. 63-70.
[17] Cf. Lauren Fasullo, "What About the Word Kephale ('Head') in the New Testament?" A study presented to Grace Bible Fellowship, Baton Rouge, LA. http://searchingtogether.org/kephale.htm

Endnotes Cont'd:

[18] Joy Bussert, *Battered Women*, LCA, 1986, p.6. *Cf.* Murray J. Harris, "A Comparison of Immortality in the New Testament with Immortality in Plato," *Raised Immortal: Resurrection & Immortality in the New Testament*, Eerdmans, 1985, pp. 201-205.

[19] Jann A. Clanton, *In Whose Image? God & Gender,* Crossroad, 1991, p. 41. "Underlying the Victorian notion of ladies' frailty was an ancient conceptualization of the female that entered European scholastic tradition with the Greeks," and then "received the stamp of Christian orthodoxy when Thomas Aquinas accepted the Aristotelian position" (Alice B. Kehoe, "The Shackles of Tradition," *The Hidden Half: Studies of Plains Indian Women*, P. Albers & B. Medicine, eds., University Press of America, 1983, pp. 56-57).

[20] Bussert, p.7.

[21] *Cf.* Elizabeth A. Clark, *Jerome, Chrysostom & Friends*, Edwin Mellen Press, 1982, 254pp.

[22] Rosemary R. Ruether, *New Woman, New Earth*, Beacon, 1995, pp.17-18.

[23] Bussert, p. 7.

[24] *Ibid.*, p. 9.

[25] *Ibid.*, p. 12. *Cf.* Del Martin, "An Overview of Cruelty," *Battered Wives*, Pocket Books, 1977, pp. 29-32.

[26] *Ibid.*

[27] Cited by Bussert, pp. 11-12.

[28] *Banner of Truth*, #81, June, 1970, p. 1.

[29] Coline Jenkins-Sahlin, "The Women's Declaration," *33 Things Every Girl Should Know About Women's History*, Tonya Bolden, ed., Crown Publishers, 2002, p. 19.

[30] "Challenge of Women's Liberation," *Cross & Sword: An Eyewitness History of Christianity in Latin America*, H. McKennie Goodpasture, Orbis, 1989, pp. 264-267.

[31] Eerdmans, 1986, pp. 33-34; *cf.* pp. 73ff., 90ff.

[32] *Outrageous Women, Outrageous God: Women in the First Two Generations of Christianity*, E.J. Dwyer, 1996, p. 165.

[33] Ana De Campos, "Liberation," p. 266.

CHAPTER 7

IS PAUL CONCERNED ABOUT WOMEN TEACHING?

"But I am not now permitting a woman to teach with the goal of getting her way with a man, but to be in quietness."

TRADITIONAL VIEW:

1 Timothy 2:12 is used as an always-binding *command* by Paul that women are not to teach men, which, if done, would wrongfully usurp male authority. Instead of teaching, women are to be and remain in silence.

CORRECTIVES:

First, it must be pointed out that there is no command [imperative] from Paul in this text. The wording in the King James Version, "I suffer not a woman," can certainly sound like a command in English, but it isn't so in the original Greek text. Instead, it is a simple present tense, "I am not now permitting a woman...." This tense use could imply a shift in Paul's strategy that arose because of the local and unique problems that existed in Ephesus, which focused on the socio-economic presence of Artemis' Temple. Timothy had worked with Paul for years and was probably not used to hearing restrictions on the sisters coming from Paul. But now Paul announces, "I am not now permitting a woman...."

Considering the background of the assembly in Ephesus will be helpful in this regard. Read Acts 18:24-20:1 and you'll see that Paul spent three years there. So far as we know, this was his longest tenure in any city during his journeys. With this in mind, we can surmise that during his years in Ephesus —approximately A.D. 54-57— the sisters were functioning along with the brothers in a fashion similar to the meeting described in 1 Corinthians 14. It was not Paul's habit to put restrictions on the sisters. However, things changed when false teaching crept in and some believers, including an unknown number of women, were involved in the aberrations, some of which no doubt involved the Artemis cult. As a result, some six years after he left Ephesus [approximately A.D. 63], Paul must announce to Timothy, "I am not now permitting a woman to teach...."

After leaving Ephesus, around A.D. 58 Paul came to the island of Miletus [30 miles south of Ephesus] and called for the elders of the Ephesian assembly. In his farewell address to these servants, Paul mentions no concerns about the sisters, but does warn them, "I know that after I leave, savage wolves will come in among you and will not spare the flock. Even from among yourselves people will arise and distort the truth to draw away disciples after them" (*cf.* Acts 20:29-30). It appears that by A.D. 63 this had come to pass, and Timothy was left in Ephesus to correct the confusion created by false teachers and false teaching (*cf.* 1 Tim.1:3-4).

Paul wrote a letter to the Ephesian assembly around A.D. 61. This epistle is the pinnacle of Paul's sublime expression of God's purpose in Christ and his Body, but there are no concerns expressed in it about the sisters nor are any restrictions on them mentioned in his apostolic communication.

Around A.D. 64-65, Christ himself directed a short letter to the Ephesian assembly which is recorded in Revelation 2:1-7. Jesus expressed his concerns to them, but such correctives had nothing to do with the functioning of the sisters. This is significant because in Jesus' letter to Thyatira he was upset about the false teaching ministry of a woman nicknamed "Jezebel" (*cf.* Rev. 2:20ff.).

Two infinitives. When Paul says, "I am not now permitting a woman," he follows with a *neither...nor* construction involving two infinitives, *didaskein* [to teach] and *authentein* [to have one's way with, to dominate]. It must be asked, how do these two infinitives correlate? Philip Payne and others suggest that the best fit is that of *goal* or *purpose.* In other words, Paul in this Ephesian situation where some women were propagating error does not want them to teach with the purpose or goal of getting their way with [or dominating] a man. Payne sees the closest English parallel to how these two infinitives are employed to be our idioms: hit 'n' run, eat 'n' run, hence, teach 'n' dominate—to teach with the goal of dominating [with false teaching]. *It is this specific type of teaching that Paul is not permitting.*[34]

There is only one use—and let me emphasize that it is the *single instance*—of the verb *authenteo* in the New Testament and it is the infinitive *authentein* in 1 Timothy 2:12. Traditionally it has been translated as, "nor to usurp authority over the man." This view assumes that the very act of a woman teaching a man is inherently a wrongful deed that violates male headship. But nowhere is there a shred of Biblical substantiation for such an extreme position. From both Testaments we glean the active role of women as presenters of God's will to his people:

> • Deborah, a prophetess, judge and wife, sat by her palm tree and made judgments as men and women came to her for counsel in applying the Mosaic law to their lives (*cf.* Judg. 2:16-19; 4:1-5:31).

> • King Josiah sent a male envoy to the prophetess and wife Huldah after the Book of the Law was discovered. She gave them [and ultimately, Israel] the word of the Lord (*cf.* 2

Kings 22:14-20; 2 Chr. 34:22-28).

• Priscilla and Aquila explained the way of God more perfectly to Apollos in their home in Ephesus (*cf.* Acts 18:19-26). The assembly in Ephesus also met in the home of Priscilla and Aquila where we can only assume that she had some very edifying things to say.

• When males and females prophesy in a gathering, Paul says that "learning" is one of the outcomes. Thus, brothers and sisters are constantly learning from one another. In this sense, it is clearly not wrong for women to contribute to the "learning" [manthano] of males.

If there is a divine law that women-teaching-men is sinful, then there can be no exceptions. But there is no concern in this regard expressed in Scripture, and there are clearly cases where women taught men. In Romans 12:6-7 where Paul is listing some gifts, he mentions "prophesying" and "teaching." There are no gender restrictions here—both men and women can be involved in such activities. *There is nothing inherently wrong with women-teaching-men, but it is a problem when women teach error, or teach in an attempt to get their way with men. Of course, the same concerns hold true if males teach error or teach with the goal of dominating others!*

But the vital matter that must be reckoned with is that *authentein* simply does *not* have the meaning "exercise authority over." In classical Greek literature before Christ, the word was used to refer to a *murderer* or to one *who contracted for a murder to take place.* Linda Belleville observes:

> If Paul had wanted to speak of an ordinary exercise of authority, he could have picked any number of words. Within the semantic domain of "exercise authority," biblical lexico-graphers J.P. Louw and Eugene Nida have twelve entries, and of "rule" [and] "govern" forty-seven entries. Yet Paul picked none of these. Why not? The obvious reason is that *authentein* carried a nuance [other than "rule" or "have authority"] that was particularly suited to the Ephesian situation.... [Louw and Nida] put *authenteo* into the semantic domain "to control, restrain, domineer" and define the verb as "to control in a domineering manner": "I do not allow a woman...to dominate a man" (*cf.* 1 Tim. 2:12).... . [They] also note that [*authentein*] is expressed idiomatically as "to shout orders at"...or "to bark at".... So there is no first century warrant for translating *authentein* as "to exercise authority" and for understanding Paul in 1 Timothy 2:12 to be speaking of the carrying out of one's official [teaching] duties. Rather the sense is the *Koine* [common Greek] "to dominate; to get one's way."[35]

We must remember that our Lord taught us that in his kingdom "authority"—who's in charge—is to be a *non-issue* (*cf.* Matt. 20:24-28; 23:11; Mark 9:34; Luke 9:46; 22:24). The idea of one person having dominion over another or others is the essence of all that is antichrist; it is clearly how the world operates and, as a pattern of behavior, is one which we are encouraged to diligently avoid, based on the life and teachings of Jesus, the Christ. No one is to be the top-dog, and there are no positions of authority. I don't know how many times I've heard, "women shouldn't be in positions of authority." *The truth is, neither males nor females are to be in positions of authority!* There is no human chain-of-command in Christ's domain. The greatest position is at the bottom of the ladder. Those with the most spiritual influence will live as those with no authority. They will live as slaves and children—who had no status in first century culture. The greatest in Christ's kingdom lays down his life for others—which is precisely what Jesus did as the servant *par excellence.*

By his example, then, we must rid ourselves of the traditional idea that some kind of inherent authority resides in the position of "teacher" [or, in our day, "preacher"]. Christ is the one with all authority in his kingdom, and he oversees his assemblies by his word and Spirit. Everything that is brought before the brethren is weighed and evaluated in light of the truth as it is in Jesus. Hebrews 5:12 says, "by this time you ought to be teachers, [but] you need someone to teach you

the elementary truths of God's word all over again."
Obviously, not every person has the gift of teaching
(*cf.* James 3:1), but all the brothers and sisters can be
teachers in some way and contribute to the learning
process in the assembly. Again, the New Testament
is not against women teaching, but Paul does put the
kibosh on a woman teaching with the goal of *dominating*
a man, which was the specific problem in Ephesus.

It is crucial to understand that the only place in
the New Testament where the word "authority" is
directly connected to gender is in 1 Corinthians 7:1-7.
Interestingly, in this passage the "authority" [*exousia*]
mentioned has *nothing* to do with the husband bossing
the wife around. Instead, it is a *mutual authority*— neither
the man nor the woman has "authority" over their own
body. The wife has authority over her husband's body,
and the husband has authority over his wife's body. An
implication of this truth is that the two cannot separate
from one another physically unless they mutually agree
[*symphonou*, be in symphony] that this should be done.
Many take "male headship" to mean that the husband
has "the final say." But how could that be in light of
1 Corinthians 7:1-7? The husband, Paul teaches here,
should not unilaterally announce, "We are going to be
physically separated awhile." Such action should only
take place *if they mutually agree on it.* If this is the case in
an important issue like physical separation, one would
assume that the goal in marital decision-making is for
the couple to be *one-minded.* In light of this passage

what "male headship" actually entails needs to be reexamined.[36]

The evidence we have examined leads to this conclusion: *in 1 Timothy 2:11-12 Paul did not issue a universal restriction that applies to all believing women in all Christian gatherings; instead, he responded to the specific problems in Ephesus with gospel perspectives.* Craig Keener thus rightly observes:

Other passages in Paul which clearly demonstrate his approval of women's ministry of God's word indicate that 1 Timothy 2:9-15…cannot prohibit women's ministry in all situations, but is limited to the situation in Ephesus and perhaps some other congregations facing similar crises in this period of the church's history.[37]

Endnotes:
[34] Philip Payne, "*Authentein* in 1 Timothy 2:12," Evangelical Theological Society Seminar Paper, Atlanta, Ga., November 21, 1986.
[35] Belleville, "Usurping," pp. 211, 216.
[36] *Cf.* Appendix Three, "What About 1 Cor. 7:1-5?," *et passim* in the Review Article of John Piper's *What's the Difference?*
[37] "*Man & Woman*," *Dictionary of Paul & His Letters*, IVP, 1993, p. 591.

Women...After a period
of independence
that came with the spread
of Christianity,
...were relegated
to a lower order....
[T]he more feminine
liberty was suppressed,
the more women were accused
(of being the temptress
of Genesis, etc.),
[and] the more they were
reduced to silence.

—Jacques Ellul

CHAPTER 8

WHY NOTE THAT ADAM CAME FIRST?

"For Adam was first formed, then Eve."

TRADITIONAL VIEW:

The creation of Adam before Eve shows that women are subordinate to male headship. Paul refers to the creation order to reinforce why it is wrong for women to teach men.

CORRECTIVES:

There is no evidence in the pre-fall account of Adam and Eve's creation, or in 1 Timothy 2:12, that a wife's subordination to her husband is in view. Nowhere does Scripture teach that all women must submit to all men. The concepts of "head" and "submit" coupled together apply specifically and solely to the marital relationship (*cf.* Eph.5:22-24).

Keep in mind that Eve was already in Adam's side before her appearance on earth. The name "Adam," in fact, includes Eve—"When God created Adam, he made him in the likeness of God. He created them male and female and blessed them. And when they were created, he called them 'Adam'" (*cf.* Gen. 5:1-2). This was a type of Christ and his bride. Just as Adam fell into a deep sleep when his wife came forth from his side, so Christ descended into the sleep of death and when his side was pierced, out of him flowed his bride into the ground to die with him. Later she would become the firstborn of a new creation, also with him, by him and in him.

We tend to think of that which is "first" as being the most important, as being superior, or as having priority. But Paul's use of "first…then" "does nothing more than define a sequence of events or ideas… . This, in fact, is the case throughout Paul's letters [and the New Testament, for that matter]. 'First-then' defines a temporal sequence, without implying either ontological or functional priority."[38] Thirteen verses later Paul says, "let the deacons *first* be proven, *then* let them serve…" (*cf.* 1 Tim. 3:10). Why Paul would mention Adam being made first is highlighted by noting the female-centered religion in Ephesus.

Reflecting on the background of the Ephesian assembly will be helpful at this point. The Temple of Artemis was a massive structure and was the focus of religious and business attention in Ephesus. Her Latin name was Diana. Her temple "was 230 feet wide and 426 feet long, with a roof supported by 127 columns, each 6 feet in diameter and 65 feet tall."[39] The effects of this woman-centered religion, while hardly unique, were pervasive. The predominant share of cash flowing through this city was connected to the sale of idols and religious objects, temple prostitution, temple-based "money-changers" and the sale of divine favors —not to mention the associated revenues drawn from food consumption, rents from housing visitors and all the usual things done to satisfy tourists.

Paul and his associates were in Ephesus for three years. It is likely that some of the converts to Christ were women whose work had been in and around the cult of Artemis, including prostitution. Many of the ladies having grown up in Ephesus would be skewed to a female-centered outlook on religion. The gospel influence reached the point where many believers were confessing their past evil activities and burning their occult books publicly (*cf.* Acts 19:18-19). A riot almost erupted because at stake was the financial welfare of the community couched in terms of honoring their female goddess —"Artemis is the goddess that everyone in Asia and the whole world worships".... They all shouted the same thing for two hours: "Great is Artemis of Ephesus" (*cf.* Acts 19:27, 34). N.T. Wright provides this excellent summary of religion in Ephesus and the "why" of Paul's instructions in 1 Timothy 2:11-15:

> There are some signs in the letter that it was originally sent to Timothy while he was in Ephesus. And one of the main things we know about religion in Ephesus is that the primary

religion—the biggest temple, the most famous shrine—was a female-only cult. The Temple of Artemis [that's her Greek name; the Romans called her Diana] was a massive structure which dominated the area; and, as befitted worshippers of a female deity, the priests were all women. They ruled the show and kept the men in their place.

Now if you were writing a letter to someone in a small, new religious movement with a base in Ephesus, and wanted to say that because of the gospel of Jesus the old ways of organizing male and female roles had to be rethought from top to bottom, such that the women were to be encouraged to study and learn and take a leadership role, you might well want to avoid giving the wrong impression. Was the apostle saying, people might wonder, that women should be trained up so that Christianity would gradually become a cult like that of Artemis, where women did the leading and kept the men in line? That, it seems to me, is what verse 12 is denying. Paul is saying, like Jesus in Luke 10, that women must have the space and leisure to study and learn in their own way, not in order that they may muscle in and take over the leadership as in the Artemis cult, but rather so that men and women alike can develop whatever gifts of learning, teaching, and leadership God is giving them.[40]

Such background material aids our understanding of 1 Timothy 2:9-15 at least in the following ways:

• It shows why Paul connected female prayer with modesty in verse 9. Some women had come out of the Artemis religion, which included public sexual displays, and this would account for dressing habits that could be far from modest. We know that female Artemis followers sought her blessings by coming into her presence with fancy hair, bedecked with jewels and ornate clothing.

• This provides the rationale for understanding why a woman coming out of and influenced by the Artemis cult could raise conflicting false teachings which would involve the goal of "dominating a man."

• We can then appreciate why some women, raised under the Artemis-cult practices, would be in need of the exhortation regarding learning in quietness.

• "Adam was formed first" had a real punch with Artemis in the background. The Artemis-cult taught that Zeus and the Titaness Leto had twins and the female came first—Artemis originated before Apollo. The Apollo-cult was the dominant form of religion in the Greek world at the time. It is not surprising, then, that there would be competition between those who derived their livelihoods from the female-based Artemis-cult and the greater number of more-obviously male dominated Apollo-cult worshippers.

• This can help explain why Paul stressed that Eve was "deceived." Paul punctured the Artemis balloon in two ways —Adam was made first, not woman; Eve was not superior to man for she was deceived into sinning against God.

• Verse 15 is mysterious indeed, but the Artemis backdrop provides needed light. We can thus understand why Paul would mention help in childbirth through faith in Christ. The women in Ephesus looked to Artemis for help during the childbirth process. "As the mother goddess, Artemis was the source of life, the one who nourished all creatures and the power of fertility in nature. Maidens turned to her as the protector of their virginity, barren women sought her aid, and women in labor turned to her for help."[41]

Endnotes:

[38] Belleville, "Usurping," p. 220.

[39] Ames, "Modest Dress..." p. 7.

[40] "The Biblical Basis for Women's Service in the Church," an address given at St. John's College, Durham, England, at the CBE Conference, Sept. 4, 2004. It is not true that the Artemis-cult consisted of all female priests. It is now believed that the controlling priests were males working "behind the scenes" putting subjugated women forward into performing roles of "temple priestesses." Certainly the purpose of the temple was the economic welfare it brought to the city and those who ran the city [males]. This would be the first century version of an adult theme park.

[41] Belleville, "Usurping," p. 220.

CHAPTER 9

WHAT ABOUT EVE BEING DECEIVED?

"But the woman being deceived became a transgressor."

TRADITIONAL VIEW:

Verse 14 shows that serious problems arise when women take the lead. Paul does not want women to teach because they are more easily deceived than men. Women are more prone to wander into error. Therefore, the teaching role is to be left in the hands of males.

CORRECTIVES:

Central to the flawed idea that women are more prone to error is a key assumption—that females are inferior to males when it comes to spiritual discernment. Yet the entire history of the church—in which women were removed from the picture—illustrates beyond question that males are every bit as susceptible to conjuring up, propagating and falling into error. Most false teaching has originated with and been spread abroad by males during the last two millennia.

"Isn't Paul using Eve as an example of what can go wrong when women usurp the male's leadership role?.... This view is without scriptural support. Eve was not deceived by the serpent into taking the lead in the male-female relationship. She was deceived into *disobeying* a command of God, namely, not to eat the fruit from the tree of the knowledge of good and evil. She listened to the voice of false teaching and was deceived by it."[42]

The notion that females are more capable of being deceived than males is shown to be false by observing that Paul applies the Eve-deceived model to an entire Christian congregation (*cf.* 2 Cor. 11:3). The possibility of being deceived is not a problem peculiar to females.

"The language of deception calls to mind the activities of the false teachers at Ephesus. If the Ephesian women were being encouraged as the superior gender to assume the role of teacher over men, this would go a long way toward explaining 1 Timothy 2:13-14. The Christ-centered relationship between the sexes was not intended to involve female domination and male subordination. But neither was it intended to involve male domination and female subordination. Such thinking is native to a fallen creation order (*cf.* Gen. 3:16)."[43] Why would we want to take our cue from the curse-ridden words, "your desire will be your husband, and he will rule over you" (*cf.* Gen. 3:16)? That is a simple description of sin's implications for the husband/wife relationship. Wouldn't we want to be informed instead by the redemptive implications of Christ's cross and resurrection, and the pre-fall relationship of Adam and Eve to which Jesus appeals in Matthew 19:4-6?

It is fascinating to take note of the parallels between 1 Timothy 2:11-15 and Revelation 2:20-24:

• Paul – "I am not now permitting a woman…." Jesus to Thyatira—"You permit the woman… ."

• Paul – "to teach with the goal of dominating a man… ." Jesus to Thyatira—"she teaches…my servants to commit fornication… ."

• Paul – "the woman [Eve] being deceived…." Jesus to Thyatira—"she deceives my servants…."

• Paul – "she will be delivered through childbearing if they remain in faith… ." Jesus to Thyatira—"I will cast her ['Jezebel'] into a bed…and I will kill her children with death."

As I pointed out earlier regarding Revelation 2:20-24, Jesus' problem is not that a female was teaching, but that she was a false prophetess whose teaching was causing the Lord's servants to sin. The implication would be that Jesus had no issue with male and female prophets exalting Christ in the assembly. If it was the apostolic custom for sisters to be silent, then one would expect the Head of the assemblies to sternly rebuke such a fundamental violation of decorum by this woman "Jezebel." Apparently, Jesus did not see this as a gender issue, but as a concern for *what* was taught and the *effects* the teaching had on the hearers.

Endnotes:
[42] Belleville, "Usurping," p. 223.
[43] Ibid.

CHAPTER 10

THE GOSPEL APPLIED TO CULTURAL SITUATIONS

A major protest often expressed by some is that if you don't believe that 1 Timothy 2:9-15 is a timeless universal restriction on women, then you are on a slippery slope leading to truth becoming a wax nose. Is this a valid concern?

The New Testament letters were written with reference to specific problems that occurred across various local assemblies, often with differing cultures. Steve Atkerson observes, "Everything in the New Testament is called an 'occasional document.' There was some occasion, usually a problem, that motivated the author to write the book."[44] What is wrong, then, in noting that in 1 Timothy 2:9-15 Paul brought timeless gospel truth to bear on a specific situation in Ephesus? Here is a summary of how that truth was applied:

• Usually the sisters and brothers functioned together in the participatory meetings of the assembly. Because of false teaching that had infected some women, Paul announced that some should be learning in quietness, not teaching with the goal of dominating men.

• It is simply not right for *anyone* to teach with the goal of dominating others. In Christ's kingdom no one is to dominate anyone else. "You are all brethren." No clergy. No laity. No honorific titles. No elevation of some above others. If anything, give honor to the parts least esteemed. Nowhere in the NT is this mandate overturned.

• The Genesis mandate to have dominion over the earth was given to *both* Adam and Eve. They were not to seek dominion over each other, but to carry out their stewardship of the earth as a team. This Scriptural perspective counters the idea that females are superior to males which was probably taught in the Artemis religion of Ephesus.

• Just as Eve had been deceived by the serpent's false statements in the Garden, so some women in Ephesus were deceived by the false teaching that was making the rounds.

• Many women in Ephesus looked to the goddess for help and guidance regarding the issues of virginity, fertility and childbirth. Paul directs godly women to look to the Lord Jesus.

The truth is, in most cases we have just bits and pieces of information about what was behind many apostolic statements in the epistles, just as we have only incomplete ideas of what happened in a particular historical setting. Often it is hard to know exactly what question was being answered or what problem was being addressed. We are, as it were, hearing one side of a conversation. But such issues do not keep us from either profiting from the New Testament, or discerning the Lord's mind. The Holy Spirit teaches us the mind of Christ. However, we do have to confess in humility that it will always be a struggle to properly understand many portions of Scripture.

There are cultural matters in the New Testament which we have to face. In 1 Corinthians 11:1-16, for example, you have some gospel perspectives brought to bear upon some cultural issues like head-coverings. Some people conclude that head-coverings are still binding; others see them as a cultural item that we are not required to emulate in our day. 1 Timothy 2:8 mentions men praying with uplifted hands. Do we teach that male prayer is invalid unless the hands are lifted up? Would 1 Timothy 2:9 lead us to confront a sister who donned some jewelry that contained some pearls or gold? Based on 1 Timothy 5:9, would we tell a 57-year old widow in need that we couldn't help her for three years until her 60th birthday? Why don't we "greet one another with a holy kiss" (*cf.* 1 Thes. 5:26)?

The New Testament was written in the first century

and many local and culturally-rooted issues appear on its pages. Because of this are we to conclude that it is all "cultural" and contains no relevant "truth" for us today? No, rather we affirm that the gospel is brought to bear on many Jewish and Gentile cultural matters that impacted the early Christian assemblies.

As we, being New Covenant believers, approach any topic or concern, the key perspective for us must be, "you have heard him and have been taught in him, just as truth is in Jesus" (*cf.* Eph. 4:21). The fundamental truth about sisters in Christ *is that they are free to function.* There is no revealed emphasis on universally applicable restrictions to their service in the kingdom.

Endnote:
[44] *In Search of the Biblical Church, DVD,* Tim Germain, ed., 2007.

CHAPTER 11

CONCLUSION & SUMMARY

Evidence cited here suggests that the traditional understanding of 1 Timothy 2:11-15 rests on some very shaky assumptions, and some fundamental misunderstandings about what Paul actually said. Difficulties found in these texts are often glossed over by those desiring to use them to muzzle female ministry. It is time for honest Bible students to revisit 1 Timothy 2:11-15 and to separate reality from fiction. Those who simplistically wave 1 Timothy 2:12 as a proof-text to silence women had better be careful that they do not incur the dreaded millstone by hurting Christ's little ones (*cf.* Matt. 18:6; Mark 9:42; Luke 17:2).

In terms of what actually happened in history, I think Bart Ehrman puts his finger on another huge factor in the marginalization of women in the church —*the movement from simplicity to institutionalization.*

Women played a prominent role in Paul's churches, as missionaries and leaders; moreover,

Paul maintained that in Christ the distinctions between male and female were obliterated. But Paul did not advocate a social revolution for women; instead, he insisted that men and women maintain their distinctive gender roles.... Women may have enjoyed more prominent roles in the Christian communities early in the movement's history because churches met in the home, women's sphere of influence. When churches acquired a more public character, however, men appear to have asserted more fully their gender claims and removed women from positions of authority.[45]

SUMMARY:

1. *1 Timothy 2:11-15 says nothing about women being or remaining "silent."*

2. *There is no command [imperative] in 1 Timothy 2:12 connected to women not teaching. Paul uses a simple present tense, "I am not now permitting...."*

3. *The infinitive, authentein, does not mean "to exercise authority over." The two infinitives, didaskein and authentein, are best correlated together as purpose or goal, thus translated as "I am not now permitting a woman to teach for the purpose of getting her way with a man."*

4. *Some key elements in 1 Timothy 2:11-15 are clarified and elucidated by considering the pervasive influence of* *the Artemis cult in Ephesus: (a) women in Ephesus sought the favor of Artemis by offering prayers as they appeared before her donning expensive clothing, jewels, and fancy locks; Paul indicates that such gaudy attire and presentation are unnecessary for Christian women; (b) the need for a posture of learning on the part of some women because of the influence of false teaching; (c) the female-centeredness of the Artemis religion is suggestive of why a woman could teach with the goal of dominating a man; (d) because it was believed that Artemis came first from Leto and then her male twin Apollos was born, it can be understood why Paul would point out that Adam was formed first; (e) because women were exalted in the Artemis-cult, it can be appreciated why Paul would mention that Eve was deceived into sin; (f) while many women looked to Artemis in connection with fertility and childbirth, Paul directs godly women to Christ as the promised Seed who was promised to Eve in Genesis 3:15.*

5. *When the ekklesia began on the Day of Pentecost the very first thing Peter mentioned concerned males and females prophesying together. Women and men prophesying are mentioned by Paul in 1 Corinthians 11:4-5. In 1 Corinthians 14 Paul wished for prophecy —from the whole assembly— to be central. Thus, to use 1 Timothy 2:11-15 as a basis to completely silence the sisters in Christian assemblies is hardly an accurate way to handle Scripture. It uses one context to cancel out the revelation of many others.*

6. *In light of these findings, those who persist in using 1 Timothy 2:11-15 as a means of subordinating women in the body of Christ may be guilty of continuing in and perpetuating a false teaching.*

It is safe to say that it is the perception of most Bible-believing people that 1 Timothy 2:11-12 raises red flags concerning female ministry. I hope that this study has successfully demonstrated that such a perception is ill-founded, groundless and unnecessary. May we have grace and humility to search the Scriptures together in order to see what is indeed really so!

Endnote:
[45] *The New Testament: A Historical Introduction to the Early Christian Writings*, 3rd Ed., Oxford, 2004, p. 406.

APPENDIX ONE

The Ephesian Social World
Providing the Backdrop
for Paul's Teaching in 1 Timothy

[The following is an email from Dr. Frank R. Ames, Director of Library Services and Professor of Medical Informatics at Rocky Vista University, Parker, CO. He spoke on 1 Timothy 2:11-15 on August 11, 2007, at the Christians for Biblical Equality conference in Denver. I sent him my article on 1 Timothy 2, and this is his response.]

Dear Jon:

Thank you for sending a draft of your article on 1 Timothy 2. I enjoyed reading it, though was saddened to learn about the dismissal of Sheri Klouda. I was not aware of her situation so took time to read more about her plight *(http://kerussocharis. blogspot.com/2007/01/sheri-klouda-gender-discrimination_17.HTML)*.

Regarding your article, I think that your references to Artemis Ephesia advance the argument in the right direction, and I think that they can be nuanced and expanded. Artemis worship does provide the informing background for the whole of 1 Timothy, for the Ephesian Christians once worshipped Artemis or, at the very least, were significantly influenced by the city culture devoted to Artemis. The author of the epistle seems to be combating mixed devotion to Jesus, whom the converts had embraced, and to Artemis, whom the converts could not yet abandon altogether. Although the epistle does not mention Artemis by name, its allusions to Artemisian beliefs and practices would not have been missed or misunderstood by citizens of Ephesus. In another epistle, when Paul reports that he "fought wild beasts at Ephesus" (*cf.* 1 Cor. 15:32), he surely refers to his conflict with Artemis worshippers, for the Ephesian goddess was known as "Artemis the Hunter, Queen of the Wild Beasts" (*Iliad* 21.470). I offer only a few other examples, though many may be identified in 1 Timothy.

1. The first doxology in the epistle is directed "to the only God," and the language implies that the author of the doxology has a competing deity in mind (1:17). The concluding doxology reiterates the concern in the description "who alone has immortality and dwells in unapproachable light, whom no man has ever seen or can see" (6:15-16a; *cf.* 2:5). Artemis was, of course, known as Phosphorus or light-bearer (Strabo, Geo. 3.1.9), who carried

her torch through the forests but could never be approached (*cf.* Also "savior," "immortal," "invisible").

2. The promise of being "saved through child-bearing" (2:15) counters Ephesian belief that Artemis was the goddess who protected women in labor. Interpretations of (2:15) concluding that it refers to a life of caring for children or to the birth of Jesus are simply unaware of the social context of the Ephesian people, or the mortality rates and concerns of ancient women. This promise directly confronts reliance upon the protection of Artemis. Fearing death during the dangers of labor, women throughout the ancient world and particularly in cities with shrines to Artemis turned to her for safekeeping. Artemis was a perpetual virgin who discouraged marriage and often punished pregnant women at the time of delivery by inflicting death.

3. The call for appropriate prayers that is found in 1 Timothy 2 also counters Artemisian worship practices. Men sought her for help in battle; women petitioned her for protection in childbirth. This, I would argue, is why the epistle instructs the men to pray for peace and why it admonishes women to dress modestly: both instructions are about traditional Artemisian prayer practices.

To recognize the unified argument throughout 1 Timothy 2, one need only the minor prompting of a few inscriptions or statements from classical literature. I quote two from *The Greek Anthology*: "The head covering and light blue veil of Amphareta rest on your head, Goddess of Childbirth, because she promised to give them when she asked you to keep dreaded death far away during labor;" and "Goddess, Savior of Children, accept and keep this bridal cloak and the glossy, plaited crown from my head, Blessed Goddess of Childbirth, from Tisis, who remembers how you guarded her when she felt the pains of labor" (VI, 270; VI, 274).

In Ephesus women prayed to Artemis by offering elaborate clothing and adorned braids of hair, whereas the men prayed by raising hands slightly above waist level with palms turned upward. Regarding these women, Heliodorus wrote, "Their locks of hair carry prayers" (*Aeth*. 1.12).

Other aspects of Artemis worship are evident in references to shipwreck, savior, false widows [a class of devotees of Artemis], instructions to marry, respect for leaders, and warnings against greed. Regarding the creation of Adam and Eve reference, the analogy is the birth of Artemis and Apollo, for Artemis was born first.

I think that you have spotted a crucial cultural/

religious dynamic at work in the epistle. Perhaps some of these other details will prove useful in solving a few remaining interpretive issues in the letter.

With my regards,

Frank Ritchel Ames

When my daughter, Kelli,
said her bedtime prayers,
she would bless every family
member, every friend,
and every animal
(current and past).
For several weeks, after
we had finished the nightly
prayer, Kelli would say,
"And all girls."
This closing soon became part
of her nightly routine.
My curiosity got the best of me
and I asked her,
"Kelli, why do you always
add the part about 'all girls'?"
Her response, "Because everybody always finishes their
prayers by saying 'All Men'!"

—Anonymous

APPENDIX TWO

New Light on 1 Corinthians 14:34-36
Would Paul Call the Speaking of Women "Lewd" & "Filthy"?
A Summary by Jon Zens, July 2007

In "The Elusive Law," Cheryl Schatz presents evidence demonstrating that verses 34-35 are not Paul's words, but the remarks of some in Corinth based on the *Talmud's* restrictions on women (DVD #4, *Women in Ministry: Silenced or Set Free?, MM Outreach*, Nelson, B.C., Canada, 2006).

I've been wrestling with the issues raised regarding women in 1 Corinthians 11-14 for twenty-six years. My first article, "Aspects of Female Priesthood," appeared in 1981. For the first time I feel as though significant light has broken through the lingering problems and questions. Without doubt every conceivable explanation of what is entailed in 1 Corinthians 14:34-35 can be challenged from some angle. It is admittedly a difficult passage. However, the position convincingly set forth by

Cheryl does the best job I've ever seen of doing justice to what the verses actually say and the immediate context, beginning in 1 Corinthians 11.

For a long time I've wondered what "law" was in view in verse 34. There is strong reason to believe that it is not the Old Testament, but the *Talmud* that is being cited. According to Wikipedia, "*The Talmud* is a record of rabbinic discussions pertaining to Jewish law, ethics, customs and history." In Jesus' day the first part of the *Talmud*, the Mishnah, was in oral form, but in A.D. 200 and 500 it and the Gemara were put into writing. It is crucial in order to understand what follows that, even before Christ's life, the traditions of the elders had largely supplanted Moses as the principal source for conservative Jewish legal and spiritual interpretation. It was, in other words, extra-biblical teaching created by an entrenched and politically motivated religious bureaucratic hierarchy. In brief, two key issues point to why the Jewish oral law [*Talmud*] was behind what was stated in vv. 34-35.

1. *Only the Talmud silences women.*

2. *Only the Talmud designates the speech of women as "shameful."*

THE TALMUD SILENCED WOMEN

Cheryl observes that "The silencing of women was a Jewish ordinance. Women were not permitted to speak in the assembly or even to ask questions. The rabbis taught that a woman should know nothing but the use of her distaff."

Josephus, a Jewish historian, asserted that "the woman, says the law, is in all things inferior to a man. Let her accordingly be submissive."

The Talmud clearly affirms the silence of females:

"A woman's voice is prohibited because it is sexually provocative" (*Talmud, Berachot* 24a).

"Women are sexually seductive, mentally inferior, socially embarrassing, and spiritually separated from the law of Moses; therefore, let them be silent" (summary of Talmudic sayings).

THE TALMUD CALLED THE VOICE OF A WOMAN "SHAMEFUL"

"It is a shame for a woman to let her voice be heard among men" (*Talmud, Tractate Kiddushin*).

"The voice of a woman is filthy nakedness" (*Talmud, Berachot Kiddushin*).

The English translation of the Greek word, aiskron, as "shameful" or "improper" hardly conveys the strength of what the word encompasses. The affirmation in v. 35, Cheryl notes, is that a woman's speaking is "lewd, vile, filthy, indecent, foul, dirty and morally degraded."

Male and female prophesying was inaugurated on the day of Pentecost (*cf.* Acts 2:17-18). Paul approved the prophesying of women in 1 Corinthians 11:5. In 1 Corinthians 14 he saw the whole body involved in prophesying—"everybody is prophesying" (v. 24), "each one of you has a teaching" (v. 26), "you may all prophesy one by one" (v. 31). How could the same apostle Paul a few pen strokes later turn around and unequivocally designate women's speech in the body as "filthy, lewd and vile"? It makes no sense at all. I have always felt that verses 34-35 didn't sound like Paul. Something was awry.

The matter is greatly cleared up with the realization that Paul did not write the negative words about women in vv. 34-35. Instead, those basing their view of women on the oral law did. Paul never required women to be silent and never called female speaking "lewd and filthy." *The Talmud* was guilty of advocating both.

This is further confirmed in v. 36 when Paul exclaims "What! Did the Word of God originate with you?" The "What!" indicates that Paul is not in harmony with what was stated by others from the *Talmud* in vv. 34-35. *Thayer's Lexicon* notes that the "What" is a disjunctive conjunction "before a sentence contrary to the one just preceding, to indicate that if one be denied or refuted the other must stand."

Sir William Ramsay commented, "We should be ready to suspect that Paul is making a quotation from the letter addressed to him by the Corinthians whenever he alludes to their knowledge, or when any statement stands in marked contrast either with the immediate context or with Paul's known views."

Paul contrasts his commands which promote edification by the varied contributions of all with the restrictive prohibitions upon women demanded by the anti-gospel *Talmud*. Paul saw the voices of the sisters as a vital part of the building up of the Body of Christ. *The Talmud*, on the other hand, viewed female voices as "shameful" and as "filthy nakedness."

We know that various concerns and questions came to Paul from the Corinthians in a letter. He refers to this communication several times in 1 Corinthians. If quotation marks are placed at the beginning and end of vv. 34-35, thus seeing them as the words of some Corinthians to Paul, the apparent contradiction between Paul's encouragement of female participation and then his seeming silencing of them is resolved satisfactorily. This is even more obvious when we recall that Paul would not have used quotation marks in his writings. Why? They had not been invented yet!

Those who use 1 Corinthians 14:34-35 as a basis for requiring the sisters to be silent in the meetings would do well to consider the strong possibility that the words they cite as proof-texts are completely non-Pauline; rather, they reflect the non-gospel viewpoint of the *Talmud*. Are they prepared to maintain, as the anti-feminine *Talmud* did, that a woman's voice is "dirty" and "like filthy nakedness"? I submit that it is unthinkable that Paul would assign such awful sentiments to the sisters' words.

I would encourage you to obtain this set of 4-DVD's which contain 3.5 hours of instruction. They are filled with insight and presented in a respectful, Christ-like spirit. You may not be persuaded by every point that is suggested, but you will be challenged to search the Scriptures to see what is really so.

HELPFUL EXCERPTS:

The following excerpts are take from Joanne Krupp's *Woman: God's Plan Not Man's Tradition*, Preparing the Way, 1999, pp. 80-83.

[used with the permission of the author]

The Context of 1 Corinthians 14:34-36

What does the rest of 1 Corinthians tell us that will shed light on these verses?

We know the Corinthian Christians had written Paul a letter (7:1) and that in that letter a number of issues were raised that Paul needed to address.

In Paul's letter, as he addressed a question or issue that had been raised by the Corinthians in their letter to him, sometimes he simply referred to the subject in question, and then responded to it, as in the following examples:

> 1:11 – For it was declared to me about you, my brethren, by the ones of Chloe, that there are strifes among you...

> 7:1 – Paul says, "now concerning the things about which you wrote..."

7:25 – now concerning virgins...

8:1 – now concerning things sacrificed to idols...

9:1 – he asks questions to bring up the next subject, "Am I not free?" "Am I not an apostle?," etc. He is obviously referring to their questions regarding his being called an apostle.

12:1 – now concerning spiritual gifts...

Other times Paul repeated the Corinthians' erroneous statements and then proceeded to correct, or bring balance to, their thinking.

6:12 – Paul seems to be quoting them— "All things are lawful for me," then he counters with "but all things are not profitable." Then he repeats again what probably was their statement to him, "All things are lawful for me," and again balances that statement with, "but I will not be mastered by anything." The Corinthians were justifying their license by their words because Paul had taught, "You are not under law, but under grace."

The portion in question here, 1 Corinthians 14:34-35, finds Paul describing in some detail how the gifts of the Holy Spirit are to be in operation in a church assembly, and specifically the gift of prophecy. At this point a new subject is being introduced. Paul seems to shift to the subject of women in the assembly.

It is very much in keeping with the pattern of this letter for Paul, in verses 34 and 35, simply to be repeating the words of the Corinthians,

"Let the women keep silence in the churches; for they are not permitted to speak, but let them subject themselves just as the law also says. And if they desire to learn anything, let them ask their own husbands at home; for it is improper for a woman to speak in church."

What follows in verse 36 seems to rebut their statement when he says, "What! Was it from you that the Word of God first went forth? Or has it come to you only?" Then he closes this chapter with a few more remarks concerning prophecy and speaking in tongues.

WHICH LAW?

The key phrase in verse 34 is "just as the law also says." Remember, Paul was an educated man. He called himself a Pharisee of the Pharisees. Certainly he knew the law. There is no Old Testament law or Scripture that either silences women or subjects them—none whatsoever. Check the cross reference notes in your Bible for verse 34, and you'll find no cross reference in the Old Testament. Rather, Psalm 68:11 says, "The Lord gives the command; the women who proclaim the good tidings are a great host."

Does Paul have the right to silence that "great host of women"? Inconceivable!

However, the Jews were living according to the *Talmud*, not according to the Old Testament Law. Remember the *Talmud* contains regulations and traditions that had become more important than the Old Testament book of the Law.

In the "Ten Curses of Eve" listed in the Babylonian *Talmud*, the sixth is summarized this way:

"He shall rule over thee," the wife being in total submission and subjugation, since the wife is the personal property of the husband.[1]

When he quotes their statement back to them in verses 34 and 35, which makes reference to the law,he is attempting to show them that they are still living and operating by the oral law of the Jews or Jewish traditions.

> The German lexicographer, Schleusner, in his Greek-Latin Lexicon, declares that the expression "as also saith the law" refers to the Oral Law of the Jews. Here are his words: "The oral laws of the Jews or Jewish traditions...in the Old Testament no precept concerning the matter exists," and he cites Vitringa as showing that it was "forbidden by Jewish traditions for women to speak in the synagogue."[2]

Paul would never have made such a statement as is quoted in verses 34 and 35 attributing something to Old Testament law that simply did not exist. Not only that but all through his letters he tried to free believers from the bondage of the law, not hold them to it (*cf.* Rom. 6:14; Gal. 2:16, 5:1).

By Paul's response in verse 36, he is saying, "Who do you think you are, setting yourselves up to proclaim something as from God that is not supported by Scripture?"

We are doing Paul a disfavor and discrediting his intelligence by accusing him of originating this statement rather than understanding that he was simply quoting theirs. Paul is not attempting to establish the silencing of women in the New Testament Church. On the contrary, he is chiding the Corinthians for their attempt to keep women silent and thereby prevent them from freely ministering as the men were free to do.

Endnotes:

[1] Charles Trombley, *Who Said Women Can't Teach?* (North Brunswick, NJ: Bridge Publishing, Inc, 1984), p. 30. Summarized from *Genesis with a Talmudic Commentary* by Herson.

[2] Johann Friedrich Schleusner, as quoted in Katherine Bushnell, *God's Word to Women* (privately reprinted [ca. 1976] by Ray B. Munson, P.O. Box 417, North Collins, NY 14111, [originally published] 1923), p. 201.

APPENDIX THREE

"In the Lord, however..."
1 Corinthians 11:11
Sorting Out Crucial Gender Issues

A review article of *What's the Difference? Manhood & Womanhood Defined According to the Bible*, John Piper, Crossway Books, 2001, 91pp.

By Jon Zens, December, 2009

While we were on a ministry trip going as far south as Oklahoma City, a good friend gave me *What's the Difference?* and asked me to comment on it. After reading it, I felt that the content begged for more than a cursory response. What follows, then, is my attempt to biblically reflect upon some of many issues raised in this book.

In this little book, John Piper distills his understanding of gender "differences as God wills them to be according to the Bible" (p. 14). He is not interested in getting bogged down in numerous technicalities which are dealt with in other larger sources he lists. However, as he boils things down to what he sees as important essentials, some serious flaws are revealed.

This book contains some solid wisdom, but several of the author's key assumptions and conclusions about the Bible and gender appear not to give full weight to all that the Scripture sets before us. By exposing some critical fallacies in Piper's approach, it will become clear that much more thought needs to be given concerning manhood and womanhood than is provided in his book.

WHAT ABOUT 1 CORINTHIANS 7:1-5?

It is interesting that in Piper's major publication, *Recovering Biblical Manhood & Womanhood* (1991), there are separate articles devoted to Ephesians 5:21-33, 1 Corinthians 11:3-16. Colossians 3:18-19, 1 Peter 3:1-7, etc., but 1 Corinthians 7:1-5 is suspiciously absent. Likewise, in *What's the Difference?* there are two lists of verses provided that deal with marriage, but once again 1 Corinthians 7:1-5 is not included (pp. 21, 66).

This omission is unfortunate for the following reasons. First, 1 Corinthians 7:1-5 is the *only* place in the NT where the word "authority" [Greek, *exousia*] is used with reference to marriage. But it is not the authority of the husband over the wife, or vice versa, that is in view, but rather a *mutual authority* over each other's body. 1 Corinthians 7:4 states that the wife has authority over her husband's body. One would think that this would be a hard pill to swallow for those who see "authority" as resting only in the husband's headship.

Secondly, Paul states that a couple cannot separate from one another physically unless there is *mutual consent* [Greek, *symphonou*]. Both parties must agree to the separation or it shouldn't happen. There is in this text, then, nothing supporting the contention that the husband's "authority" should override his wife's differing viewpoint.

John Piper suggests that "mature masculinity accepts the burden of the final say in disagreements between husband and wife, but does not presume to use it in every instance" (p. 32). But 1 Corinthians 7:5 challenges Piper's assumed maxim. If the wife disagrees with a physical separation, the husband should not overrule his wife with the "final choice" (p. 33). Biblically, such separation can occur only if both husband and wife are in "symphony" [unity] about such an action.

Now if *mutual consent* applies in an important issue like physical separation from one another for a period of time, wouldn't it seem proper that coming to one-mindedness would be the broad decision-making model in a healthy marriage? Piper feels that "in a good marriage decision-making is focused on the husband, but is not unilateral" (p. 32). In light of 1 Corinthians 7:1-5 I suggest that decision-making should focus *on finding the Lord's mind together*. Over the years the good ideas, solutions to problems and answers to dilemmas will flow from both husband and wife as they seek the Lord as a couple for "symphony."

1 Corinthians 7:5 throws a wrench into the works for those who would conclude that the husband has the "final say" under presumed authority commonly known as "male headship." Paul teaches that unless the couple can agree on a course of action, it should not be executed. I suggest that this revelation invites us to re-examine what the husband's headship really entails (*cf.* Gordon D. Fee, "1 Corinthians 7:1-7 Revisited," *Paul & the Corinthians: Studies On A Community in Conflict*, Trevor J. Burke/J. Keith Elliott, eds., Brill, 2003, pp. 197-213).

"CONCERNING CHRIST AND THE EKKLESIA," EPH. 5:32

What burdens me as I listen to the contemporary rhetoric surrounding the issue of marriage and the roles of husbands and wives is that the typological nature of marriage is minimized or omitted. This arises because most believe that marriage is fundamentally an institution or creation ordinance started in the Garden of Eden. Yet it seems quite clear that earthly marriage is a type—a picture of Christ and his bride, the *ekklesia* (*cf.* Eph.5:31-32). So to talk about marriage as isolated from the typology of Jesus and his church is to miss a Christ-centered perspective. Marriage is given real meaning and significance only when it is vitally connected to its purpose as an earthly picture of Christ and his people. We must not sever what God has joined together. Consider these beautiful parallels:

Before the fall into sin, "Adam" as the first human being was looked upon by the Lord as "male and female." Genesis 5:2 makes the astounding, but crystal clear observation that "When God created Adam he made this one in the image of God. Male and female he created them, and he blessed them and named them Adam when they were created." Adam looked like one person, but he was actually a plurality—he had a woman within his body. "He named *them* [plural] Adam [singular]."

The Lord Jesus is called "the last Adam" (*cf.* 1 Cor. 15:45). He looked like one person, but he, too, had a bride in his side. He came to purchase the *ekklesia* of God with his own blood (*cf.* Acts 20:28). The unity between Christ and his people is so deep that to touch his flock is to touch the Savior himself—"why do you persecute me?" (*cf.* Acts 9:4).

Adam was put to sleep in order that his wife might be created. "And the LORD God caused a deep sleep to fall on Adam, and he slept." Adam was completely passive in the creation of his wife.

Likewise, Christ was put to sleep in order that his wife might be created. She could not become his bride without being saved from her sins. Her redemption required that Christ be put to the sleep of death as her substitute. Christ's death was a part of his passive obedience to God. He took upon himself the death His bride deserved.

Adam's side was opened, and his wife was made from that which was removed. "And [God] took one of [Adam's] ribs, and closed up the flesh in its place. Then the part which the LORD God had taken from man He made into a woman."

Likewise, Christ underwent an opening of his side and from what came forth redeemed his wife. "But one of the soldiers pierced His side with a spear, and immediately blood and water came out." The church of God was redeemed with this blood, and birthed through this water.

Interestingly, Eve is pulled from the "side" of Adam. The Hebrew for "side" is *tsela* and the Greek is *pleura*. When Jesus died it was his "side" (*pleura*) that was pierced with a spear, and from that redemptive act the church is, as it were, pulled forth as a new Eve (*cf.* John 19:34; 20:20, 25, 27).

Adam was married to his wife: "and [God] brought her to the man. And Adam said, 'This is now bone of my bones and flesh of my flesh; she shall be called Woman [Hebrew, *Ish-shah*], because she was taken out of Man [Hebrew, *Ish*].' Therefore a man shall leave his father and his mother and be joined to his wife, and they shall become one flesh."

Likewise, Christ is married to his wife. As Eve was united to Adam in the most intimate of physical relationships, so is the church united to Christ in the most intimate of spiritual relationships. Adam and Eve were united into "one flesh." Christ and his church are united into "one body." She is therefore called "the church which is His body" (*cf.* 1 Cor. 12). And as God designed the union of husband and wife to last a lifetime, so the union of Christ and his church will last forever. Nothing will ever separate the bride from the love of the heavenly Bridegroom.

We discover another parallel in this: as a man leaves his father and mother in marriage on earth so he can cleave to his wife, so Christ left his Father in heaven to come to earth, redeem his people through his death, burial and resurrection, and so cleave to his Bride forever.

From a biblical perspective, specifically in God's promise in Genesis 3:15, *it can be said that the whole unfolding of human history is ultimately about the coming of Jesus the heavenly Groom who secured the forgiveness of sins and the fellowship of his Bride*—folks from every people group on earth, a people so great in number that no one can count them. We are given, by the apostle John in the Book of Revelation, these glorious descriptions of the end of history:

For the wedding of the Lamb has come and his bride has made herself ready. Fine linen, bright and clean, was given her to wear.... . I saw the Holy City, the New Jerusalem, coming down out of heaven, prepared as a bride beautifully dressed for her husband... . Come, I will show you the bride, the wife of the Lamb.... . The Spirit and the Bride say, "Come!" And let the person who hears say, "Come." Those who are thirsty, let them come; and those who are willing, let them take the free gift of the water of life (*cf.*, Donald Joy, *Bonding: Relationships in the Image of God*, Evangel Publishing House, 1999, pp. 19-29; Daniel Parks, "Christ Typified in the First Marriage, Genesis 2:18, 21-24," *www.sovereigngraceofgod.com/parks. htm*).

Once we begin to see marriage as an earthly pointer to the ultimate marriage of the Lamb with his Bride, it puts the issues dealt with in *What's the Difference?* in a completely new light. The emphasis in Genesis 1-2 is not on *differentiated roles* but on a *one-flesh partnership*. The issue is not "Who's in charge?" but "How can we in our relationship enhance our love and service to God?" It's not about the "creation ordinance" of marriage. It's about a passionate relationship—"she is bone of my bone and flesh of my flesh!" This is ultimately Christ's proclamation to his *ekklesia*.

Connecting human marriage to Christ and the church also opens the door for understanding the crux issue in sexual sins. People tend to look at sexual sin as a violation of God's will—and it is. *But the most fundamental problem with sexual deviations is that they mar, violate and contradict in various ways the beauty and purity of Jesus' relationship with his Bride, the ekklesia.* Adultery, same-sex relationships, fornication, promiscuity, bestiality, rape, using women/ children/men in the sex industry, female circumcision, etc., are all destructive perversions of "the beginning" when God created them male and female, and of "the fullness of time" when Christ came to gather a Bride from all the nations.

Without sin, Adam and Eve were fully naked and had no shame. "There is now no condemnation to those in Christ" (*cf.* Rom.8:1). Sexual sins that twist the image of Christ and his Body practice all kinds of nakedness attended with the fullness of shame. They ruin and disfigure the wonder of Christ and his *ekklesia* becoming "one flesh."

EPHESIANS 5:21-33

With this "profound mystery" as a backdrop, we can better understand Paul's words to husbands and wives in Ephesians 5:22-33. In Ephesians 5:18 the apostle gives an imperative to be "filled with the Spirit," and five participles follow showing the fruit of such a life. Verse 21 sets forth the fifth evidence of the Spirit-filled community, "submitting yourselves to one another out of reverence to Christ." Here we see a *mutual submission* among all the parts of the body. This is the setting for the specific relationships that follow, beginning with husbands and wives.

Verse 22 has no verb. It reads literally, "wives to your own husbands as to the Lord." Then why do most English translations read, "wives *submit* to your own husbands..."? Because they have correctly inferred that *submission* is implied. In the English language a sentence is not complete without a verb. In the Greek, a sentence may be complete without a verb, but in such cases, the action is assumed to continue from the preceding sentence. The verb in verse 21 is "submit." The assumed verb in verse 22, therefore, should also be "submit."

But that's not the whole story. Since verse 22 was written in such a way as to make it deliberately dependent on verse 21 for its action verb, it is also appropriate to assume a continuation of any previously established qualifiers to that action. In verse 21, the act of submitting is not a one-way street, but *mutual*—"to one another." If Paul did not intend for that same spirit of mutuality to be assumed in the submission implied in verse 22, he would have supplied a new verb and structured the sentence differently. Even though Paul's focus in verse 22 is on "wives," there is no justification for stripping the implied "submit" supplied by the translators of its previously established mutuality. A wife should indeed voluntarily "submit" to her husband. But that does not cancel out her husband's responsibility to just as willingly submit to his wife. Indeed, husbands and wives should "submit to one another."

It should be clear, therefore, that Paul's motivation for instructing believing wives to submit to their husbands was not to establish a hierarchy in the marriage relationship —nor in any other relationship between believers. It is the unique, "one another" quality of life within the body of Christ that is its most essential characteristic. Just as elders [pastors] have no inherent right to lord it over those whom they shepherd (*cf.* 1 Pet. 5:3), husbands have no inherent right to lord it over their wives. In Christ, earthly marriage is an equal partnership, with both husbands and wives willingly submitting to one another as unto Christ. Paul's only reason for underscoring the wife's need for submission to her husband is because her role in marriage, as the following verses so beautifully reveal, is to be an earthly reflection of Christ's Bride, the church. And in the "oneness" of that relationship, there is neither male nor female, "for you are all one in Christ Jesus" (*cf.* Gal. 3:28).

Because of church teachings, personal leanings and cultural practices, words like "submission" and "authority" are laden with potential misunderstandings. Dennis J. Preato reminds us that we need to think things through a little more carefully:

> The Greek word, *hupotasso*, is often translated as "submitting to" or "being subject" in Ephesians 5:22. However this Greek word has more than one use and a range of meaning that is quite different from what people today generally think. "*Hupotasso*" actually has two uses: military and non-military. The military has a connotation of being "subject to" or "to obey" as if you are under someone's command. Most people would probably think of this meaning. However the non-military use means "a voluntary attitude of giving in, cooperating, assuming responsibility, and carrying a burden" (*Thayer's Greek Lexicon* #5293). In ancient papyri the word hupotasso commonly meant to "support," "append," or "uphold" (Ann Nyland, "Papyri, Women, & Word Meaning in the New Testament," *Priscilla Papers*, 17:4 (Fall, 2003), p. 6)...[W]hy would Scripture need to command Christians to be filled with the Spirit in order to be subject to, follow orders, or be under someone's authority? A person does not need to be filled with the Spirit to follow orders,

for even nonbelievers demonstrate this fact when they "submit," or obey their superiors ("Empirical Data in Support of Egalitarian Marriages & A Fresh Perspective on Submission & Authority," Presented at the Evangelical Theological Society, April 23, 2004).

The wife's responsibility is mentioned in verses 22-24 and 33. It is often overlooked that Paul directs more attention to the husband's responsibilities, as the seven verses in between are directed toward the men in the households. It is possible that Paul has more to say about the husband's responsibilities toward his wife because of the generally low status of women in the first century—they were often viewed as property.

In Ephesians 5:22-33, then, we see a beautiful picture of husbands reflecting the Lord's pattern toward their brides—sacrificial nourishing, protecting and caring—and the wives reflecting the pattern of the *ekklesia* toward her Groom—respect and submission.

WHAT ABOUT GIFTED WIVES?

Piper's view of a wife's submission seems to focus unduly on the husband's life and ministry. Wifely submission, he says, is "a *disposition* to yield to the husband's authority and an *inclination* to follow his leadership...the divine calling to honor and affirm her husband's leadership and help carry it through according to her gifts" (pp. 52,66). But with this view how does the husband truly encourage the ministry of his wife's gifts?

What's the Difference? seems unable to envision or deal with scenarios where wives have special gifts in the church. For example, Deborah was first a prophetess and then a judge. But she was called a "mother in Israel" and the name of her husband is mentioned. Likewise, Huldah was a prophetess in Israel, and a wife whose husband is also named. It is clear that a wife can be eminently gifted and express her gifts in the covenant community without tainting her marriage. The "ministry" of either husband or wife should flow out of and be subordinate to a mutually respectful [submissive] marriage relationship.

The woman's options are neither a demand to suppress her gifts for the sake of her calling as a wife, nor to express those gifts to the detriment of her marriage. She can be a good wife and still use her gifts to the fullest extent. The husband's benediction should rest upon the blossoming expression and use of his wife's gifts.

FEMALE LEADERSHIP?

When all is said and done, it seems that Piper's goal is for sisters to be eliminated from any leadership in the church. "The realities of headship and submission in the marriage have their counterparts in the church" (p. 66). He sees males at the helm of the "God-given order of leadership by spiritual men" (p. 67).

But it is not quite that simple. The New Testament indicates that women did play a part in leadership in the first century. Piper rightly sees in the verb *proistemi* [literally, "to stand in front of"] the concept of management and leadership. He sees in this word "leadership for sure" and applies it to males where it is used in 1 Timothy 3:5 and 1 Thessalonians 5:12 (p. 86). However, his limiting of leadership to men runs into a serious problem in Romans 16:2. Here, Phoebe—who delivered the Roman letter to the believers—is noted by Paul to be a "deacon of the *ekklesia* in Cenchrea" and a form of *proistemi* is used with reference to her. It certainly appears that there was some form of "leadership" attached to her functions in the Body of Christ.

In Romans 16:7 Andronicus and Junia are mentioned as "outstanding among the apostles." Some have argued that the name here is masculine, "Junias." However, the evidence points to the fact that until A.D. 1100 she was considered to be a woman, and then she was transformed by translators into a man (*cf.* Eldon Jay Epp, *Junia: The First Woman Apostle*, Fortress, 2005, 138pp.; Linda Belleville, "A Re-Examination of Romans 16:7 in Light of Primary Source Materials," *New Testament Studies*, Vol. 51, 2005, pp. 231-249).

No one would deny that some form of leadership is contained in the word "co-workers." Paul designated men like Timothy and Aquila and women like Priscilla and others as "co-workers"— these were people whose labor was associated with evangelism, church-planting and church care.

It is interesting to note that the idea of "household-leader" is used both of men and women. *Oikodespotes* [literally, house-despot] is used of married women in 1 Timothy 5:14. It should be noted, then, that in the first century a married woman was also called "master-of-the-house."

WHERE DO WOMEN "PROPHESY"?

On the Day of Pentecost it was proclaimed by Peter, citing the prophet Joel, that both men and women would "prophesy" in the Messianic age. Paul made it clear in 1 Cor.14 that "prophecy" should be central in the body gathering, where there would be participation by all (*cf.* 1 Cor. 14:23-24,26). In 1 Corinthians 11:1-5 Paul has no issue with sisters and brothers "praying and prophesying."

But Piper's view dictates that women not speak publicly in any way that might snuggle up to "teaching." Thus, his notion of what it means for a woman to "prophesy" is non-public and very limited in scope. "The fact that a Christian wife and church member, according to Acts 2:17, may 'prophesy' implies, at least, that she may often have ideas and insights that a wise and humble husband and pastor will listen to and adopt" (p. 84).

It will not do to have a double standard. If Piper's definition of prophecy applies to a woman then it must mean the same for a man. To say that a man can prophesy publicly but women non-publicly is unacceptable. Acts 2 and 1 Corinthians 11 indicate that they do it together. "Non-public" prophecy is an oxymoron. Prophecy as portrayed in the New Testament is exercised publicly in the assembly.

The issue of female prophesying highlights a most serious flaw in Piper's viewpoint. He defines men's and women's roles in such a way that he cannot let the full weight of Scripture speak. To suggest that female prophecy is summed up in a sister speaking valuable things privately to her husband or pastor is ludicrous and agenda-driven. Philip had four virgin daughters [with no husbands] who prophesied. And we are asked to believe that their ministry consisted solely in *privately* sharing some thoughts with "a pastor"! I don't think so.

REVELATION 2:20 – A PROPHETESS "TEACHES"

In Christ's words to the Thyatira *ekklesia* we find that a female prophetess was "teaching" very bad things. Christ gave her some space to repent—not of the fact that she taught, but that her teachings were errant. Just as the fact that there were false teachers in the *ekklesias* shows that there were good teachers, so the fact that there was an evil female prophetess is indicative of the reality that there were women who prophesied soundly.

The seven letters of Christ to the ekklesias give glimpses into the life of the early assemblies. It would appear that female prophetesses functioned—for both good and ill—as was the case also with male prophets/teachers.

CONNECTING THE WRONG DOTS

Piper presents one line of reasoning that is severely

flawed and consequently quite misleading. He links certain concepts and assumes that the way he puts the pieces together is accurate. But is he correct in doing this?

The realities of headship and submission in marriage have their counterparts in the church. Thus Paul speaks of authority and submission in 1 Timothy 2:11-12. We will try to show that "authority" refers to the divine calling of spiritual, gifted men to take primary responsibility as elders for Christlike servant-leadership and teaching in the church.... So when Paul puts those two things together and says, "I do not permit a woman to teach or exercise authority," one very natural implication is, "I do not permit a woman to assume the office of elder in the church." So the authority Paul has in mind in 1 Timothy 2:12 at least includes the authority of elders (pp. 66, 90).

To yank the word "authority" out of 1 Timothy 2:11-12 and connect it to "the authority of elders" is unwarranted and fallacious. The Greek word Piper links with "authority" in 1 Tim. 2 is the infinitive *authentein*, and it is only used here in the New Testament. The Timothy text has to do with restraining a woman from teaching for the purpose of having her way with a man. The translation, "to usurp authority over a man" is not accurate. Linda Belleville observes:

> If Paul had wanted to speak of an ordinary exercise of authority, he could have picked any number of words.

Within the semantic domain of "exercise authority," biblical lexicographers J.P. Louw and Eugene Nida have twelve entries, and of "rule" [and] "govern" forty-seven entries. Yet Paul picked none of these. Why not? The obvious reason is that *authentein* carried a nuance (other than "rule" or "have authority") that was particularly suited to the Ephesian situation... . [Louw and Nida] put *authenteo* into the semantic domain "to control, restrain, domineer" and define the verb as "to control in a domineering manner": "I do not allow a woman... to dominate a man"(1 Tim. 2:12)... . [They] also note that [*authentein*] is expressed idiomatically as "to shout orders at"...or "to bark at".... So there is no first century warrant for translating *authentein* as "to exercise authority" and for understanding Paul in 1 Timothy 2:12 to be speaking of the carrying out of one's official [teaching] duties. Rather the sense is the Koine [common Greek] "to dominate; to get one's way" ("Teaching & Usurping Authority: 1 Tim. 2:11-15," *Discovering Biblical Equality*, Ronald Pierce & Rebecca Groothuis, eds., IVP, 2005, pp. 211,216).

GENDER "PROBLEMS" CREATED BY A TEACHING

We've all seen examples of how errant teaching can impact people. If a person has been brought up to believe that a certain race is inferior, then he/

she will feel very awkward being in table fellowship with such people. So it would seem that Piper's teaching about manhood and womanhood creates unnecessary problems and tensions. Here are some aspects of the outworking of his views:

> To the degree that a woman's influence over man is personal and directive it will generally offend a man's good, God-given sense of responsibility and leadership, and thus controvert God's created order. A woman may design the traffic pattern of a city's streets and thus exert a kind of influence over all male drivers. But this influence will be non-personal and therefore not necessarily an offense against God's order.... All acts of influence lie on the continuum between personal and impersonal.... Some influence is very directive, some is non-directive. For example, a drill sergeant would epitomize directive influence. It would be hard to see how a woman could be a drill sergeant over men without violating their sense of masculinity and her sense of femininity.... The God-given sense of responsibility for leadership in a mature man will not generally allow him to flourish long under personal directive leadership of a female superior. J.I. Packer suggested that "a situation in which a female boss has a male secretary" puts strain on the humanity of both. I think this would be

true in other situations as well. Some of the more obvious ones would be... in professional baseball if a woman is made the umpire to call balls and strikes and frequently to settle heated disputes among men (pp. 62-63).

If mutual respect for males and females in God's image is emphasized, then a man having a female boss is not inherently a problem. The problems that can certainly arise in such contexts would result from personal baggage carried by one or both of the parties, not because there is something unnatural about having a female leader.

Perhaps many women would feel uncomfortable being in military positions where they would command men, or being a baseball umpire. The point is that such positions are not limited to men by any divine law. Some women would be qualified and very capable in these situations, and perhaps a female umpire might be a calming influence in the midst of heated disputes! Every now and then in history there was a Joan of Arc!

Men and women from Israel came out to Deborah's palm tree for counsel from God's word and no one's humanity was strained. King Josiah and his men sought interpretation and directives from Huldah and had no awkward moments because they were receiving counsel from a woman.

I submit that the views of *What's the Difference?* put unnecessary pressure on women, causing them to walk on eggshells, constantly second-guessing themselves. "Are my actions around men too personal? Are they non-personal enough? Am I being too directive? Am I non-directive enough?" Women who are always wondering if they are stepping over into some "male" territory tend to just give up and retreat into the shadows. The components of Piper's grid seem to engender bondage for sisters, not freedom.

An experience Carolyn S. Briggs had in a Midwest church captures the frustration and awkwardness many women feel in churches:

> We were Elder ruled. The Elders were the shepherds of the church and held all authority. Women could not be Elders. We were not allowed to teach men the Word of God, although we had Bible studies where we taught one another.... Finally, on Saturday morning we woke up early and met with a small group of stalwarts who wanted to study theology from the seminary textbooks Phil had supplied.... "So, Carolyn," Phil was saying. "Tell us about dispensational theology." "We can divide the history of God and man into seven dispensations and determine God's method of relating to man through each of those dispensations," I said quickly, shyly and surprised that he had called on me. I was one of only two women present. This study was really supposed to be for the men, the only ones who

could teach, according to God's Word. No one said women couldn't come, but no one especially invited them, either. "What does that mean?" Phil asked. "That sounds like God changes. We know from the Scriptures that He is the same yesterday, today, and forever." I was silent for a moment as I waited for someone else to chime in. I bit my lip and looked down. Phil laughed.... "You'd get eaten up in seminary, you know that? Stand firm, all of you. 'Study to show yourselves approved, a workman of God, unashamed.' Or in your case, a workperson," he said, winking at me. It was subtle enough. I had been put in my place, but lovingly.... I smiled at Phil and made a helpless face so he would laugh again. I didn't speak again the rest of the morning. Phil didn't call on me, and I didn't have the nerve to answer any more questions, even if I did know all of the answers (*This Dark World: A Memoir of Salvation Found & Lost*, Bloomsbury, 2002, pp. 128-129, 166, 167, 168).

Also, Piper teaches the notion that all men have some sense of "leadership" over all women. I do not think such a notion can be sustained by God's word. In terms of Biblical usage, "head" is a term used *exclusively* within marital bonds. As an example of a true masculinity that leads, provides for and protects women in general, Piper presents a scenario where a man and a woman are walking down a street and are confronted by a man with a lead pipe. "Mature masculinity," he says, "senses a natural, God-given responsibility to step forward and put himself between the assailant and the woman.... His inner sense is one of responsibility to protect because he is a man and she is a woman" (p. 41). But wouldn't he feel the same exact sense if this event happened and he was walking with another man? Isn't our sense to protect any human being rooted in the fact that both male and female are bearers of God's image? Didn't Jesus step out to protect His Bride who is both male and female?

WHAT IS "HEADSHIP"?

This is not the place to continue the debate over the meaning of "head" [Greek, kephale]. However, it does need to be noted that there is more to the story than just the simplistic assertion that kephale means to have authority over, attached to "the idea of leadership" (p. 86). There is considerable evidence that this was not the primary meaning of kephale in the first century (*cf.* "Kephale Meanings,"*http://exegetist-theberean.blog spot.com/2007/05/kephale-meanings.html*; Laurie Fasullo, "What About the Word Kephale ("Head") in the New Testament?" *http://searchingtogether. org/kephale.htm*).

The early church fathers were overall very negative toward women. Yet, as Dennis J. Preato notes, people like Cyril of Alexandria and John Chrysostom did not see *kephale* in 1 Corinthians 11 as referring to "authority over," but as "source":

Cyril:
Bishop of Alexandria (A.D. 376-444) commenting on 1 Corinthians 11:3 defines the head metaphor as "source": *Thus we say that the kephaleo of every man is Christ, because he was excellently made through him. And the kephaleo of woman is man, because she was taken from his flesh. Likewise the kephaleo of Christ is God, because he is from him according to nature* (Manfred T. Brauch, F.F. Bruce, Peter H. Davids and Peter Kaiser, Jr., Hard Sayings of the Bible, "Head of the Woman Is Man? [1 Cor. 11:3]," electronic edition).

John Chrysostom:
Bishop of Constantinople (A.D. 347-407) commenting on 1 Cor. 11:3 said the head metaphor does not mean that one has authority over another, or one is under subjection to another. Dr. Joe E. Trull, editor of *Christian Ethics Today, quotes Chrysostom: "If you think 'head' means 'chief' or 'boss,' you skew the godhead!"* (Joe E. Trull, "Is the Head of the House at Home?" [*http://www. christianethicstoday.com/Issue/009/Is %20the%20Head%20of%20the%20Ho use%20at%20Home%20(Ephesians% 205_21-6_9)%20By%20Joe%20E.%2 0Trull_009_3_.htm*], accessed 23 October, 2003) ["Empirical Data in Support of Egalitarian Marriages & A Fresh

Perspective on Submission & Authority,"
Presented at the Evangelical Theological
Society, April 23, 2004].

When we were having a Sunday gathering south of Oklahoma City (November, 2009), I presented some thoughts on marriage. In the discussion one of the couples who has been married 25 years brought out some excellent points as they talked about their relationship. The husband said that, to him, being "head" had nothing to do with "authority" over his wife, but had to do with his functioning—to use a military term—as a *point man*." This term means "to assume the first and most exposed position in a combat military formation, that is, the lead soldier/unit advancing through hostile or unsecured territory. The soldier/unit on point is frequently the first to take hostile fire. The inherent risks of taking point create a need for constant and extreme operational readiness.... The point man walks several meters out in front of everyone else and is likely to be the first one to encounter enemy soldiers. It is a hazardous position that requires alertness and ability to deal with unexpected attacks" (*en.wikipedia.org/wiki/take_point*). Another brief definition, "Point Man: lead soldier in a unit cutting a path through dense vegetation if needed and constantly exposed to the danger of tripping booby traps or being the first in contact with the enemy" (*vietvet.org/glossary.htm*).

The words of Paul in Ephesians 5 to the husbands were not about ruling over another person, but about following Christ in sacrificial actions toward their brides. All illustrations have their limitations, but "point man" does seem to capture some important images about the functions of a husband (*cf.* I. Howard Marshall, "Mutual Love & Submission in Marriage, Col. 3:18-19 & Eph. 5:21-33," *Discovering Biblical Equality*, Pierce & Groothuis, eds. (IVP, 2005), pp. 186-204).

CONCLUDING THOUGHTS:

My assessment is that *What's the Difference*? promotes its own agenda by magnifying the alleged "role" differences between men and women, and does not give proper priority to and focus on husbands and wives becoming "one" in marriage.

While John Piper claims to have "made every effort to bring the thinking of this book into accord with what the Bible teaches" (p. 14), I do not think that he succeeded, and I believe he also effectively muted much of the Biblical testimony about women. He affirms that "God does not intend for women to be squelched or cramped or frustrated" (p. 53), yet his views seem to contribute to these very tragic ends.

It would seem that in Piper's best of worlds men would accomplish the bulk of what needs to be done (pp. 60-64). What are women supposed to think when they read statements like, "it is simply impossible that from time to time a woman not be put in a position of influencing or guiding men.... The closer they get to the personal side, the more inappropriate it becomes for women to exert directive influence" (pp. 60,62)?

Felicity Dale, who was a medical doctor in England, noted that the church is *hemiplegic*— the female half of the body of Christ is paralyzed. What a tragedy! As Donald Joy observes, "We are always impoverished when a single sex group meets, discusses, and make decisions, since only one part of the full-spectrum personhood seems to be present. So where urgent decisions are being made, we surely want both sexes speaking and voting" (*Bonding*, p. 25).

Piper holds that the sisters cannot publicly prophesy (but apparently the men can). All they can do is prophesy by speaking privately to their husbands or to "a pastor." One gets the impression that gifted women like Miriam, Deborah, Huldah, Esther, Anna, Phoebe, Priscilla, Junia, and many others are left with no meaningful function in Piper's conception of *ekklesia*.

The template for gender that *What's the Difference?* lays down does not seem to be in line with the truth as it is in Jesus. The conclusion for Paul is this: "In the Lord, however, the wife is not independent of the husband, nor is the husband independent of the wife. For as woman came from man, so also man is born of woman" (*cf.* 1 Cor. 11:11). For Paul the functions of husband and wife were to be viewed from the perspective of *interdependence and respect*, not *hierarchy*.

Suggested Sources for Further Study:

Elizabeth Abbott, *A History of Celibacy*, DeCapo Press, 2001, 493 pp.

Frank Ritchel Ames, "Modest Dress, Public Silence, and Safety in Childbearing: Interpreting Paul's Instructions in 1 Timothy in Light of Ephesian Inscriptions, Artifacts, and Traditions," a paper presented at the International CBE Conference, Denver, Colorado, August 11, 2007, 17 pages (MP3).

Frank Ritchel Ames and J. David Miller, "Prayer and Syncretism in 1 Timothy," forthcoming in *Restoration Quarterly*, 25 pp.

James M. Arlandson, *Women, Class & Society in Early Christianity: Models from Luke-Acts*, Hendrickson, 1997, 238 pp.

Kenneth E. Bailey, "Women in the New Testament: A Middle Eastern Cultural View," *Evangelical Review of Theology*, 22:3, July, 1988, pp. 208-226.

Linda Belleville, "What English Translators Aren't Telling

You About 1 Tim. 2:11-15," Christians for Biblical Equality Conference, Orlando, FL, 2003 (cassette).

Linda Belleville, "Teaching & Usurping Authority: 1 Tim. 2:11-15," *Discovering Biblical Equality*, Ronald Pierce & Rebecca Groothuis, eds., IVP, 2005, pp. 205-223.

Biblical Illustrator, "Hairstyles of First-Century Asia Minor," 6:4, 1980, pp. 71-74.

Del Birkey, *The Fall of Patriarchy: Its Broken Legacy Judged by Jesus & the Apostolic House Church Communities*, Fenestra Books, 2005, 376 pp.

Manfred T. Brauch, *Abusing Scripture: The Consequences of Misreading the Bible*, IVP, 2009, 293 pp.

Peter Brown, *The Body & Society: Men, Women & Sexual Renunciation in Early Christianity*, Columbia University Press, 2008, 504 pp.

Elizabeth A. Clark, *Jerome, Chrysostom & Friends: Essays & Translations*, Edwin Mellen Press, 1979, 254 pp.

Lynn H. Cohick, Women in the World of the Earliest Christians: Illuminating Ancient Ways of Life, Baker, 2009, 352 pp.

Kathleen E. Corley, *Private Women, Public Meals: Social Conflict in the Synoptic Tradition*, Hendrickson, 1993, 217 pp.

Alan Crandall, "St. Paul Versus the Femi-Gnostics," 1996, unpublished paper, 3 pp.

Dagitim, Rehber Basim Yayin, ed. *Ephesus: Priene, Miletus, Didyma*, Revak, 1997, 96 pp.

Richard W. Dortch, *Fatal Conceit: How the Deception of Power Becomes Every Man's Trap, Every Woman's Dilemma*, New Leaf, 1993, 257 pp.

E. Earle Ellis, "*Paul & the Eschatological Woman,*" *Pauline Theology: Ministry & Society*, Eerdmans, 1989, pp. 53-86.

Eldon Jay Epp, *Junia: The First Woman Apostle*, Fortress, 2005, 138 pp.

Millard J. Erickson, *Who's Tampering with the Trinity? An Assessment of the Subordination Debate*, Kregel, 2009, 272 pp.

Lauren Fasullo, "*What About the Word Kephale* ('Head') in the New Testament?" and "A Critique of Wayne Grudem's Understanding of 'Head' in the N.T.," 1995. Studies presented to Grace Bible Fellowship, Baton Rouge, LA. *http://searchingtogether.org/kephale.htm*

Joy E. Fleming, *Man & Woman in Biblical Unity: Theology from Genesis 2-3*, CBE, 1993, 44 pp.

Gordon D. Fee, "1 Corinthians 7:1-7 Revisited," *Paul & the Corinthians: Studies on a Community in Conflict, Essays in Honor of Margaret Thrall*, Brill, 2003, pp. 197-231.

Gordon D. Fee, "Gender Issues: Reflections on the Perspective of the Apostle Paul," *Listening to the Spirit in the Text*, Eerdmans, 2000, pp. 56-76.

Gordon D. Fee, "The Great Watershed – Intentionality & Particularity/Eternality: 1 Tim. 2:8-15 As A Test Case," Hendrickson, 2006, pp. 52-65.

Matilda J. Gage, *Woman, Church & State*, Persephone Press, 1980, 294 pp.

Kevin Giles, *The Trinity & Subordinationism: The Doctrine of God & the Contemporary Gender Debate*, IVP, 2002, 282 pp.

J. Lee Grady, *10 Lies the Church Tells Women (revised and updated)*, Charisma House, 2006, 232pp.

Joseph F. Green, "Diana of the Ephesians," *Sunday School Lesson Illustrator*, 4:4, 1978, pp. 34-39.

Rebecca Groothuis, "Leading Him Up the Garden Path: Further Thoughts on 1 Timothy 2:11-15," at *www.cbeinternational.org/new/free_articles/timothy_meaning.html*

Richard Hawley & Barbara Levick, *Women in Antiquity: New Assessments*, Routledge, 1995, 271 pp.

Mary Hayter, *The New Eve in Christ: The Use & Abuse of the Bible in the Debate About Women in the Church*, Eerdmans, 1987, p.131-133, 148, 155, 161.

Anne Jensen, *God's Self-Confident Daughters: Early Christianity & the Liberation of Women*, Westminster/ John Knox, 1996, 347 pp.

Donald Joy, *Bonding: Relationships in the Image of God*, Evangel Publishing, 1999, 160 pp.

Craig S. Keener, "Man & Woman," *Dictionary of Paul & His Letters*, G.F. Hawthorne, Ralph P. Martin, Daniel G. Reid, eds., 1993, pp. 583-592.

Catherine & Richard Kroeger, *"I Suffer Not A Woman": Rethinking 1 Timothy 2:11-15 in Light of Ancient Evidence*, Baker, 1992, 253 pp.

Joanne Krupp, *Woman: God's Plan Not Man's Tradition*, Preparing the Way Publishers, 1999, pp. 97-107.

David P. Kuske, "Exegesis of 1 Timothy 2:11-15," at *www.wisessays.net/authors/k/kusketimothy*

Richard N. Longenecker, "The Sexual Mandate: Neither Male Nor Female," *New Testament Social Ethics for Today*, Eerdmans, 1984, pp. 70-93.

Dennie R. MacDonald, *There Is No Male or Female: The Fate of a Dominical Saying in Paul & Gnosticism*, Fortress, 1987, 132 pp.

L.E. Maxwell & Ruth Dearing, *Woman in Ministry: An Historical & Biblical Look at the Role of Women in Christian Leadership*, Christian Publications, 1987, 167 pp.

Berkeley Mickelsen, "Who Are the Women in 1 Tim. 2:1-15? Parts 1 & 2," *Priscilla Papers*, 2:1, 1988, pp. 1-6.

Margaret R. Miles, *Carnal Knowing: Female Nakedness & Religious Meaning in the Christian West*, Vintage, 1991, 254 pp.

Craig Morphew, "Thrown to Lions, Woman Pastor

Emerges Moral Victor," *St. Paul Pioneer Press Dispatch*, January 30, 1988, p. 3B.

John Nicholson, *Men & Women: How Different Are They?* Oxford, 1986, 193 pp.

Anne Nyland, *More than Meets the Eye: The Campaign to Control Gender Translation in Bibles*, Smith & Stirling Publishing, 2004, 131 pp.

Julia O'Faolain & Lauro Martines, eds. *Not In God's Image: Women in History from the Greeks to the Victorians*, Harper, 1973, 362 pp.

Carolyn Osiek, Margaret MacDonald, Janet Tulloch, *A Woman's Place: House Churches in Earliest Christianity*, Fortress, 2005, 354 pp.

Alan G. Padgett, "Beginning With the End in 1 Cor.11:2-16," *Priscilla Papers*, 17:3, 2003, pp. 17-23.

Philip B. Payne, *"Authentein in 1 Timothy 2:12,"* Evangelical Theological Society Seminar Paper, Atlanta, Ga., November 21, 1986.

Philip B. Payne, *Man and Woman, One in Christ: An Exegetical & Theological Study of Paul's Letters*, Zondervan, 2009, 512 pp.

Philip Payne, "Women in Church Leadership: 1 Tim. 2:11-3:13 Reconsidered," *Japan Harvest*, #4, 1981-82, pp. 19-21.

Rena Pederson, *The Lost Apostle: Searching for the Truth About Junia*, Jossey-Boss, 2006, 278 pp.

"Professor Made to Leave Seminary 'Because Women Can't Teach Men,'" *Tyler [TX] Morning Telegraph*, January 27, 2007, p. 3A.

Kathy Sanders, "Headship from a Woman's Perspective," 4th Searching Together Conference, Osceola, WI, 2004 (cassette).

Ross Saunders, *Outrageous Women, Outrageous God: Women in the First Two Generations of Christianity*, E.J. Dwyer, 1996, 182 pp.

Cheryl Schatz, "Is There A Law That Forbids Women from Teaching Men?" Women In Ministry Blog, July, 2006, at *http://strivetoenter.com/wim/2006/07/02 or www.mmoutreach.org*

"Seven Wonders of the World, Version 2.0," *Duluth News Tribune*, March 19, 2007, pp. A1, A5.

Mark Strom, *Reframing Paul: Conversations in Grace & Community*, IVP, 2000, 256pp. (especially pages 136-141; 169-180).

Willard Swartley, "The Bible & Women," *Slavery, Sabbath, War & Women: Case Issues in Biblical Interpretation*, Herald Press, 1983, pp. 178-183, 324.

Nancy Tuana, *Woman & the History of Philosophy*, Paragon House, 1992, 158 pp.

Henry E. Turlington, "Ephesus," *Sunday School Lesson Illustrator*, 4:4, 1978, pp. 40-49.

Frank Viola, "God's View of a Woman," *www.ptmin.org/ view.htm*

Frank Viola, "Now Concerning A Woman's Role in the Church," *www.ptmin.org/role.htm*

Ben Witherington III, *Women in the Ministry of Jesus: A Study of Jesus' Attitudes to Women & Their Roles as Reflected in His Earthly Life*, Cambridge University Press, 1994, 221 pp.

Jon Zens, "Exploring Paul's Concerns in 1 Tim. 2:11-15," 8th Searching Together Conference, Osceola, WI, 2007 (cassette).

Jon Zens, "Romans 16:1-16 – Brothers & Sisters Doing Kingdom Work," 7th Searching Together Conference, Osceola, WI, 2006 (cassette).

Jon Zens, "Those With the Most Spiritual Influence Live As Those With No Authority," 6th Searching Together Conference, Osceola WI, 2005 (cassette).

Jon Zens with Cliff Bjork, "Women in the Body of Christ: Functioning Priests or 'Silent' Partners?" *Searching Together*, 31:1-3, 2003, 47 pp.

Jon Zens, "Women's Ministry in Light of All That's in the Bible," DVD, East Los Angeles, July, 2009.

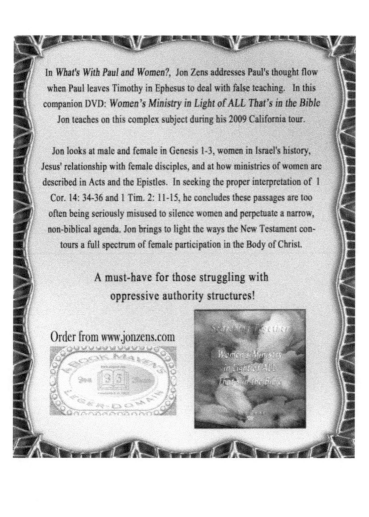

CPSIA information can be obtained
at www.ICGtesting.com
Printed in the USA
BVHW042304090322
631106BV00006B/131

Made in the USA
Columbia, SC
19 April 2022